ERNIE-ISMS

VOLUME II

Other Books by Ernie Bringas

Going By the Book: Past and Present
Tragedies of Biblical Authority (1996)

Created Equal: A Case for the Animal-Human Connection (2003)

Jesusgate: A History of Concealment Unraveled (2013, 2021)

Mexican Roots, American Soil:
A Quest for the American Dream (2016)

Ernie-isms (2022)

For summary information on these works,
visit erniebringas.com

ERNIE-ISMS

A Lifetime of Original Witticisms,
Wise Sayings, Insights, and Poems

VOLUME II
ERNIE BRINGAS

RAINBOW RIDGE
BOOKS

Cover and interior design by Frame25 Productions
Cover photograph by solarseven c/o Shutterstock.com

Published by:
Rainbow Ridge Books, LLC
Virginia Beach, VA
www.rainbowridgebooks.com

Visit the author at: erniebringas.com

ISBN 978-1-937907-77-8

Printed in the United States of America

INTERIOR IMAGE CREDITS (all c/o Shutterstock.com)
Bible: Udod Lilia | Christianity: Ihnatovich Maryia | Conspiracy Theories: berkut | Cosmic: Sloth Astronaut
| Culture and Society: NadzeyaShanchuk | Death and Afterlife: irina_angelic | Elderly: Vectors bySkop
Faith/Belief: Benvenuto Cellini | Fame and Fortune: Iconic Bestiary | Family and Friends: tynyuk | History:
Aliona Manakova | Humans: Nadya_Art | Hunting: nexusby | Hypocrisy: Ron Leishman | Justice/Judicial:
buchandbee | Knowledge and Education: PureSolution | Logic: Ilin Sergey | Love/Kindness: art_of_sun
| Marriage: Oxima | Morality and Ethics: Dirk Ercken | Mystery/Enigma: hendrikus hean | Mythology:
Chalintra.B | Nature: KrisArt | Offbeat: KingVector | Personal Diary: Omar Mouhib | Additional Poems:
Vectorry | Politics: SurfsUp | Potpourri: fields-studio | Psychology: Drawlab19 | Race: olegganko | Religion:
jaya diudara | Romance: sinna2500 | Science: Natty_Blissful | Social Media: elenabsl | Sports: Ugraphics
Trumpism: Ellagrin | Truth/Reality: Aleks_Z | War: Black Creator 24 | Women and Men: subarashii21
Young Folks: Sabelskaya

WITH GRATITUDE

A grateful thanks to my publisher Jonathan Friedman for taking on this project once again. His cover design and formatting talents are self-evident.

I want to acknowledge the wonderful work of my copy editor, Patricia Joynes. A writer doesn't always see the obvious grammar issues, and that's why an excellent copy editor is essential. She was that, and more. Aside from her many talents, e.g., photography, she's an avid animal lover and I consider her a kindred spirit.

CONTENTS

THE GIST OF IT

Written from 1959-2025, *Ernie-isms Volume ll* continues where my first book left off. Herein are an additional 893 insights, witticisms, and poems. They appear in alphabetical subject order, excepting 135 one-liners from Volume I. The title of this work, *Ernie-isms*, was not of my making, but I have embraced it nonetheless.

A few of these readings overlap in content. Accordingly, their placements should not be taken as black-and-white designations. Readers will decide their own preference in this regard.

Nevertheless, many of these comments are best suited to their assigned category. This would certainly be true, for example, under the listing classified as PERSONAL DIARY. Many of my own private feelings, shortcomings, and worldviews are apparent. But many other of my social, theological, and philosophical viewpoints are scattered throughout the other categories as well, not to mention some humorous comments sprinkled along the way.

How I interpret what I write is obvious to me but not necessarily so for the reader. I certainly know that people look at the world through their own polished lens. For that reason, a variety of emotional responses will ensue from my offerings, including those of laughter, hooray, anger, and outright disagreement (as it should be). With disagreement in mind, I will leave you with one of my poems, just to start the ball rolling.

A Penny for Your Thoughts

As sure as the night will follow the day,
You can't agree with all that I say.
Well I don't mind, I think that's good,
For we all think as right we should.

If we all thought the very same way,
We'd never see a better day.
The tree of knowledge bears no fruit,
If all we do is follow suit.

—Ernie Bringas, 2025, Phoenix/Mesa, Arizona

ANIMALS

Animal Sex, Death, and Cannibalism

The spider's realm is not so great,
When spiders try to copulate.
The widow spider kills her mate,
Unless he's quickly out the gate.

The male bee will idolize,
The queen who has a big surprise.
For when he goes to fertilize,
His big surprise is that he dies.

The female mantis having sex,
According to our latest specs,
Will seize her mate and kill him dead,
By biting off the poor guy's head.

The octopus is no exception.
He's gonna die with an erection.
He'll have some fun, but when he's done,
He's "dead in the water," and that's no pun.

1. **Animal rights**: In the observation of cruelty, a sensitive person will suffer more injury than one whose nature is not so inclined.

2. From the get-go we should strive to teach our young to have reverence for life no matter what form it takes. This is not a Pollyanna suggestion, and I know that when push comes to shove, the *necessary kill* is unavoidable. That's not the problem (albeit sad). The problem is the *unnecessary kill*. It is the thoughtless unprovoked killing of animal life that reflects the sordid tendency of our species. I am thankful for those who rise above this calloused behavior.

3. Most animals are predators, but generally they don't destroy their own kind without cause. The human animal differs. They do kill their own kind for several different reasons, many of which are unwarranted. I suppose this must be another side effect of superior intellect.

4. All carnivorous beings are serial killers.

5. When my free (uncaged) parakeet died, she was only one of many wonderful animals that I have loved and lost over the years. As I continue to age, it becomes increasingly difficult to bear that fated grief. On the other hand, I miss that loving exchange. So now the question arises: Should I choose the absence of experience to avoid the experience of absence?

6. Every creature that dies by our hand *unnecessarily*, is an affront to Providence.

7. Birds with clipped wings in small cages are another blatant symbol of a societal blind spot.

8. **Cause and effect:** When we disregard the rights and welfare of the so-called lower animals, we unintentionally impede our own well-being. From the crosshairs of the hunter's rifle to the flyswatter in the kitchen, or the neatly packaged meat at the supermarket, habitual disregard for life will inevitably backfire. The violence returns full circle because we cannot always contain deadly habits at the border of human interaction. Thus, we should not be surprised to discover that man's inhumanity to man is, in part, the by-product of man's insensitivity to other life forms.

> Most animals are
> predators, but generally
> they don't destroy their
> own kind without cause.
> The human animal differs.

9. I'm against human rights when they *needlessly* violate animal rights. When that happens, human rights become human wrongs.

10. **Thanksgiving**: We kill about 237 million turkeys for Thanksgiving each year. November is the month I go into hiding.

11. Killing any sentient life form unnecessarily, and with impunity, is the *normalization of cruelty* and, therefore, unrecognized as such.

12. Our superior intelligence blurs the commonality between us and the other mammals, but the distinction between them and us is a matter of degree, not one of difference. I know that's arguable.

13. **Holy Cow!** Sometimes I can't help myself. Yesterday, I was trying to imagine what a cow might be thinking if caught smack dab in the middle of a stampede. It must be a troublesome experience moving at a top speed of 25 mph and hemmed in on all sides. Anyway, here are 20 possibilities I thought a stampeding cow might be thinking:

"Holy Me! I'm stuck in the middle."

"I can't see a thing."

"It doesn't help being claustrophobic."

"Where the hell are we going?"

"Whose idea was this, anyway?"

"Can we slow down? I'm getting tired."

"What's the rush?" We're cows, not cheetahs."

"This looked a lot easier on *Rawhide.*"

"If we can jump over the moon, why can't we stop this stampede?"

"This is worse than a desert sandstorm."

"Where's that N-95 when you need it?"

"Where are those cattle cars? I thought we were going by train."

"I wonder how the longhorns keep from goring each other."

"I guess I'll have to go along to get along."

"Is this what they call herd mentality?"

"I hope we're not headed for a cliff."

"Oops, what did I just run over?"

"Does anyone know why we never trip?"

"Why didn't we think of this when we were being branded?"

"I hope the cow in front of me doesn't have a bowel movement."

14. **Ahimsa:** There is no living creature that is unremarkable. Life is nothing less than astonishing, whatever station it holds. In this regard, Christianity can take a lesson from Hinduism, Buddhism, and Jainism.

15. **The sacred web of life:** Those who see the interconnectedness of *all* sentient life forms will see themselves in all beings and thereby avoid the animal disregard so readily seen in others.

> "There is no living creature that is unremarkable. Life is nothing less than astonishing, whatever station it holds."

16. We are at the top of the food chain, the very top of the pyramid. If we disappeared tomorrow, the so-called lower animals would survive and thrive quite nicely. But if they

vanished, we would not survive. Point: They can live without us; we can't live without them. In this regard, we can rephrase the wording from the New Testament: So the last will be first, and the first will be gone.

> **We are not the masters of any animal; our noblest calling is to be their guardians.**

17. If we kill other animals—insects, fish, birds, cows, whatever—it should only be out of *necessity*, not out of convenience, unwarranted fear, sport, or needless dietary gratification.

13. This one puzzles me a bit. It appears through empirical observation that all sentient animals suffer. But is suffering relative? That is, does a human suffer more than a dog, a dog more than an elephant, an elephant more than a sperm whale, etc.? What about insects? And what role does intelligence play in the differing types of suffering, e.g., humans understanding the inevitability of death? But aside from the angst of foreknowledge, do all animals have the *same physical*

capacity to experience pain? I'm pretty sure that mammals do, but uncertain about the others. Hmm . . .

19. We are not the masters of any animal; our noblest calling is to be their guardians. Aside from survival needs, there are no moral grounds to think otherwise.

20. We all understand that no human has the right to infringe on the rights of another human without *justifiable* cause. However, it is a lesson yet to be learned when it comes to dealing with the so-called lower animals.

21. **Animal DNA:** The inability to see animals as family stems from how we classify them. We tend to see them as an "it" (unrelated, separate, detached, unlinked, disconnected), as opposed to recognizing them as genetically inclusive (biologically related).

(Flashback Vol. 1)
I wonder if there was a compassionate God looking out for the dinosaurs. If so, I hope it's not the same one we have.

BIBLE

Sacred Books

The Qur'an and the Bible
Are very much tribal.
But the wording within
Makes it worth their survival.

1. **"An eye for an eye"**: The 613 moral, social, and theological laws of Judaism as portrayed in the Old Testament are painted in black-and-white format (the do's and don'ts). The New Testament repainted them gray.

2. **Birds of a feather (sort of)**: Muslims do not believe that Muhammad was divine, but they do believe that his recitation of the Qur'an (received from the angel Gabriel over a period of 23 years) is God-given sacred scripture. Christians, on the other hand, have double assurance. They not only believe that the Bible is God-given, but also that the teachings of Jesus are God-given based on the belief that he was divine. *Question*: Can a statement, opinion, or teaching stand

on its own, or does it require a divine messenger, or sacred book, to make it so?

3. The Bible says that man is created in God's image. Some would argue that we have created God in man's image. Either way, God loses.

4. Most people know the biblical story of David and Goliath. However, they mistakenly think that David slew Goliath with a slingshot. But it wasn't the stone that killed the giant. If you read the story carefully, you'll see that Goliath was simply knocked cold. Thereafter, David took the giant's sword and cut off his head (I Samuel 17:51). The head rolled down to the bottom of an embankment and knocked over a few small logs (and that was the beginning of bowling).

5. The biblical Book of Ecclesiastes (1:9) states, ". . . there is nothing new under the sun." That is certainly true but for two exceptions: you and me!

6. **Fundamentalist and originalist:** To view the New Testament as a flawless revelation from God is to embrace it as an inflexible system of thought that reflects a first-century worldview. Similarly, the reluctance to amend the Constitution relegates it to a non-negotiable document—to be understood as perceived by the Founding Fathers when first written. In so doing, it becomes an unalterable system of thought that reflects an eighteenth-century worldview. In both cases, despite their invaluable reflections, these revered documents contain errors, ambiguity, and limited perspective. Cultural

beliefs frozen in time are bound to incur some measure of obsolescence. Where would we be today if we had treated all other human sources with such a fundamentalist and originalist approach?

7. Since I cannot prove or disprove the existence of God, the issue for me boils down to a matter of choice, based on what appears to be evidence within the natural order. Arguably, that proves nothing. But I lean toward the Psalms (14:1) that says, "The Fool has said in his heart, 'There is no God.'"

8. **Devil's advocate:** Are the many teachings of the Bible more important than the characters therein, even as the words of the Constitution may be more important than the men who wrote them? Either way makes a good argument.

9. In the Old Testament Book of Leviticus (19:18), we find the first mention of the great commandment to "love your neighbor as yourself." It reappears in the New Testament several times: "You shall love your neighbor as yourself." But sometimes we treat others with more understanding and kindness than we do ourselves. So, if you reverse the order of that commandment, further insight can be derived: *You shall love yourself as your neighbor.*

10. **The unpardonable sin:** Why does God expect us to forgive those who transgress against us (Matthew 6:12) when he's not willing to forgive those who transgress against him (Matthew 12:31-32)?

11. I believe in the truth of Scripture, but I don't believe that everything in Scripture is true. In different words, I take most of it seriously, but not all of it literally. If I did, I would have to believe in talking donkeys, witches, the subjugation of women, slavery, and that gays are an abomination to God, and other time-related beliefs. Belief in the absolute authority and literal interpretation of what are termed sacred books has led Jews, Christians, and Muslims into the bowels of death and destruction. History, and current events, are replete with examples. Fortunately, there are level-headed followers who make critical course corrections when their comrades veer into the extremes. Unfortunately, religious extremism remains scandalous.

12. **Matthew 5:8:** If it's true that only "the pure in heart shall see God," then no one will.

13. A story changes with each person that tells it. It changes again with each person that hears it and retells it. The significance of this tendency goes far beyond everyday gossip. Both oral and handwritten traditions prior to the invention of the printing press were significantly altered through centuries of transmission. No handwritten manuscripts, religious or otherwise, have been immune from that adulteration. That's a fact, not an assumption; we have century-old copies for comparison that prove the point.

14. For most people, even after the Enlightenment of the seventeenth century, the New Testament genres of story, history and myth remained intertwined as one. Consequently, New

Testament mythology continues to be conflated with history in a literal sense, as opposed to its parabolic teaching. The inability to untangle these conflated components has created a serious stumbling block for a proper understanding of the text, while alienating a more enlightened public.

> " The Bible says that man is created in God's image. Some would argue that we have created God in man's image. Either way, God loses. "

15. According to the Bible, blasphemy against the Holy Spirit is the unpardonable sin (aka the eternal sin). You can be forgiven for any diabolical sin imaginable, except this one. This dire warning is found in several books of the New Testament, including the Gospels of Matthew, Mark, and Luke. The central meaning of this proclamation centers on the individual's willful and final rejection of spiritual apprehension as defined by traditional Christian theology (mainly, God's plan of salvation by way of Jesus). In that narrow sense, I find the concept to be unacceptable because it ignores the honest pursuit of those who seek to understand the mysteries of life from a different intellectual or spiritual perspective. Thankfully, progressive Christians agree.

16. People often say that "tomorrow is never promised." But neither is today. The biblical Book of Proverbs (27:1) says it well: "Do not boast about tomorrow, for you do not know what a day may bring."

17. **Tongue in cheek:** According to the Book of Matthew, "Blessed are the peacemakers for they shall be called the children of God." On the other hand, blessed are the troublemakers, for without them there would be no peacemakers.

18. Many Christians embrace and proclaim the outdated beliefs of that "old time religion," even though prominent scholars of religion have uncovered insurmountable facts that contradict those traditional views. This knowledge gap between scholar and devotee is, in part, the result of the layperson's erroneous belief that the teachings of Bible and Church are unquestionable authority. Hmm, I wonder where they got that idea?

19. The Bible says we are created in the image of God. Some would argue that we have created that perception through self-aggrandizement. There is no doubt that humans display flashes of holiness and unholiness. Where does that leave us?

(Flashback Vol. 1)
When someone quotes a scripture to "prove" a point, there are usually other scriptures in diametrical tension.

CHRISTIANITY

Apostates?

Am I on the road to perfection,
Or am I on the road to defection?
They say when you give up tradition,
You'll be on the road to perdition.

Me thinks they are wrong on this topic,
And me thinks they are also myopic.
'Cause the god of my own understanding,
Is a God who is not so demanding.

I've broken away and I'm free,
So I'll just let the Mystery be.

1. The first Christian to be murdered by other Christians was a bishop named Priscillian (385 AD). He and five of his followers were put to the sword on the charge of heresy. One of the charges against him was for praying while naked. Don't ask.

2. Although Jesus taught an alternative message to his people, he was born a Jew, lived as a Jew, and died as a Jew. In today's world, this leads us to one of the most troubling and nonsensical oxymorons . . . . an antisemitic Christian.

3. **Splash!** Religious liberals will dive into the deep end of the religious pool in search of theological reality, albeit with the risk of drowning. In contrast, if you're a fundamentalist at the knee-deep end of the pool, you'll feel secure standing on your own two feet, albeit in shallow water. Question: Is it better to be at the deep end of the religious pool where traditional faith is challenged, or at the shallow end where honest inquiry may be lacking? Perhaps somewhere in-between is the optimum choice (known in Buddhism as the "Middle Path"). Or, in our case, the middle splash.

4. How do you think Jesus would greet the immigrants coming across our southern border? Aside from providing some loaves and fishes, what do you think he would tell us to do? Oh wait, I think he already did that. (Note: This is not to suggest open borders.)

5. *Vetting our sources is extremely important.* But even our gold-standard authorities are not infallible. Consider the prestigious Oxford dictionary and the comments written about Constantine the Great. Quote: "He was the first Roman emperor to be converted to Christianity and in 324 made Christianity the empire's state religion." That statement is not entirely factual. Although Constantine did elevate Christianity above all the other religions of his time, he did not declare

it to be the state religion. That did not occur until around 380 under Theodosius I (also called Theodosius the Great). *Bottom line: Sometimes it is in our best interest to double vet our sources.*

6. A minister friend of mine, while vacationing in Italy, wanted to visit a *Passionist* monastery (a religious group established in the early 1700s). Misjudging travel time, he arrived too late in the evening to enter the monastery compound. There was, however, a doorbell and a note on the entrance gate that read: "If you're here after hours, please press the button to arouse the Passionate Fathers."

7. Jesus tells his disciples: "I will make you fishers of men." I've always thought that was an odd metaphor when you consider what happens to fish when they get caught.

8. **The perfect storm:** When a Category 5 personality (Jesus), a Category 5 religion (Judaism), a Category 5 civilization (the Roman Empire), a Category 5 worldview (mythology), and a Category 5 charismatic missionary (the Apostle Paul) converge, what is the result? The result is a "divine" savior and a worldwide religion. Was this outcome caused by a coincidental merging of category 5 events, an act of God, or a combination thereof? Hmm . . .

9. **The Goldilocks zone:** When the Apostle Paul says that man alone is the glory of God, that's misleading. When he says that woman is nothing more than the glory of man, that's untrue (but this attitude was the norm for his time). He finally gets it right—albeit only in spiritual mode—when

he emphasizes gender equality: ". . . there is no longer male and female." NOTE: For the most part, prominent scholars of religion credit Paul with gender-equality attitudes within the social order. We can see in the biblical record that he elevated women to high-ranking leadership positions in his developing churches. Furthermore, based on literary DNA, many scholars have shown that gender biased verses were not likely penned by Paul.

10. **The doomsday motivator:** Some inmates on death row who await execution convert beforehand. In such cases, that impulse is driven by the prospect of impending doom. The need and urgency for a speedy conversion is not so obvious for those who are not in peril. I suspect the insightful words attributed to Jesus relate to that theme: "Those who are well have no need of a physician, but those who are sick."

11. **One extraordinary life:**

1. His mother was told by a heavenly figure that her son would be divine.

2. His birth was accompanied with supernatural signs.

3. He was recognized as a spiritual authority in his youth.

4. As an adult, he went from village to village, preaching the good news.

5. He gathered disciples around him who were amazed at his teachings and flawless character and were convinced that he was the Son of God.

6. He performed miracles . . . healing the sick, casting out demons, and raising the dead.

7. He was placed on trial before the Roman Authorities.

8. Even after his death, he appeared to his followers; they talked with him and touched him.

9. Thereafter he ascended bodily into heaven.

I suspect you have not heard of this first-century miracle-working Son of God whose name was Apollonius of Tyana (contemporary Turkey). He lived around the same time as Jesus, and both shared similar stories. However, there is no evidence that Christians formulated the Jesus story based on the life story of Apollonius, or vice versa (although their followers accused each other of doing so). Some scholars believe it is more likely that they both borrowed from the mythic hero model so prevalent in that day. However, there is no evidence to support that view. Cause-and-effect speculation is based primarily on the fact that several "Son of God" stories permeated the Mediterranean world when Jesus lived. Even the first emperor of Rome, Augustus, was called *divi filius*, "Son of the Divine." (*The Apollonius details are from NT scholar Bart D. Ehrman.*)

12. Some religious beliefs become dispensable or modified in the face of advancing knowledge and new experience. This

path of uncertainty is a never-ending process of deconstruction and reconstruction, a never-ending process of recalibration. The path of uncertainty will fly in the face of those who require the path of certainty. Either way, let's remember that there's more than one trail that leads to the mountain top.

13. Jewish and Christian biblical scholars know that the Jews never thought of the coming Messiah—the prophesied deliverer of the Jewish nation—as someone who was destined to die for the sins of the world. That was an innovative Christian concept about Jesus, and a nonstarter in Jewish theology. The "dying for sin" motto came into vogue during the writing of the New Testament to explain why Jesus died a humiliating death contrary to messianic expectation. Dying for the sins of the world was not Old Testament prophecy fulfilled.

14. **2024:** During the bitter presidential campaigns, I saw a tv ad that read: "Jesus loved the people we hate." With all due respect, Jesus didn't know the people we hate. But the ad's point is well taken since the flawed nature of human beings remains virtually unchanged, and there is no doubt that the Jesus persona represents the highest example of human virtue. (For the record, I don't hate anyone, although I'm prone to dislike some.)

15. Advancing knowledge has always been a critical component in our quest for enlightenment. Scholars of religion, for example, have discovered that the early development of Christianity was contentious, and sometimes chaotic. Also, the flawed transmission of the New Testament down through

the centuries has proven to be most revealing. I said revealing, not disqualifying. Admittedly, this will require some doctrinal and historical renovation. However, that's par for the course; there's nothing new about the need for maturing reconstruction in all fields of thought.

> " Advancing knowledge has always been a critical component in our quest for enlightenment. "

16. **Christian nationalism:** The United States national motto as printed on our currency is: "In God We Trust." During WWI, the German soldier's belt buckle was inscribed: "Gott mit uns und wir mit ihm!" (God is with us and we with him.) *Aside from our earliest notions, nationalism and gods, by their very definitions, are incompatible when merged into one.* This is reminiscent of our earliest Gospel, Mark 12:17, "Render to Caesar the things that are Caesar's, and to God the things that are God's."

17. Often, Christian faith is custom made and based on affluence or the lack thereof. The difference in belief between an American living high on the hog, and the unfortunate person born in Sudan, can be diametrical. The lens of prosperity and the lens of poverty, along with racial, gender, education,

civil wars, and geographical factors, are uniquely influential in shaping different worldviews. Religions of the world are equally pronounced in their differences, even though they share some common values. Deity perspectives are wide-ranging and sometimes irreconcilable. What lessons can we learn from this religious incongruity?

18. I've heard Christians say that it's better to believe than not, because you have everything to gain if you're right, and everything to lose if you're wrong. The problem with this thinking is that the hereafter is not a given. You may have plenty to lose in this world if you place *all* your bets on the supposed next one. In other words, "A bird in the hand is worth two in the bush." *Bottom line:* The present life should be seriously prized.

19. Many conservative Christians claim that liberal/progressive scholars of religion are trying to poke holes in the Christian tradition and the biblical text. Scholars of religion, using the scientific method while invoking analytical thinking, are not trying to poke holes into anything. They are simply uncovering the holes that are already there.
(*See also Religion*)

(Flashbacks Vol. 1)
The Jesus peril: If you promote a new principle that conflicts with the herd, beware of the stampede that ensues.

Perhaps evolution is the hand of God working in slow motion.

CHRISTIANITY (PRAYER)

The Power of Prayer Has no Power Without Faith.

1. Most prayers, it seems to me, are perfunctory or performative. Prayers whispered superficially will go no further than the stone walls of one's personal castle. Even without traditional format, to be genuinely concerned about someone is a prayer—and that concern will echo to the very edges of the universe and beyond.

2. I don't believe in prayer. But I believe in the power of prayer. That's a distinction without clarification. I leave that to your interpretation.

3. It's been said that "Nothing fails like prayer." That's because religion was never meant to be an insurance policy against hardships, and certainly not against the slings and arrows of the natural order. However, I find wisdom in the words of priest Gregory Boyle: "God protects me from nothing but sustains me in everything."

4. It matters not if prayers of petition are sincere. The gods do not prevent civilizations, tribes, cultures, empires, or the like, from collapsing, much less fulfilling the common requests of everyday living. Statistically speaking, we know that everyone is equally subject to the fortunes and misfortunes of life. Nevertheless, it seems that the quality of life is uplifted in the community of prayer. Hmm . .

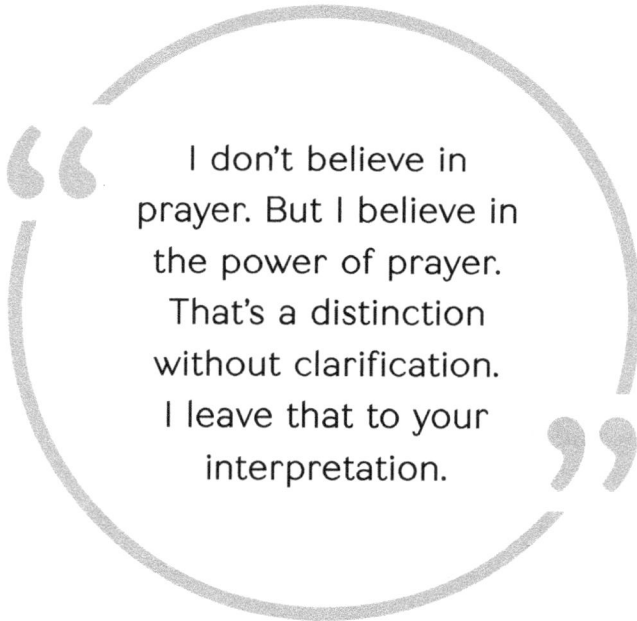

> " I don't believe in prayer. But I believe in the power of prayer. That's a distinction without clarification. I leave that to your interpretation. "

(Flashback Vol. 1)
I believe there's nothing sweeter or more powerful than a mother's prayer—even if the universe be godless.

CONSPIRACY THEORIES

Gullible

The world isn't round.
It's really quite flat.
And Elvis lives on.
You can't argue with that.

1. Extremists can cherry-pick the facts and then spin them beyond rational limits, albeit not recognized as misleading by the misinformed layperson. Of course, none of us consider ourselves to be misinformed.

2. **Why conspiracies thrive**: A logical argument based on a faulty premise will be just as convincing as one based on a viable one.

3. It is unfortunate that many idiotic conspiracies are considered logical for lack of discernment.

4. **The real cause of global warming:** Did the Earth weigh less before it was populated by humans? Think about that—8 billion people on the planet is a lot of extra weight, and the population explosion isn't helping. According to some scientists, it is human weight that is the main cause of global warming, not greenhouse gas emissions as previously thought. The problem is exacerbated by the billions of us (about 80%) who live on the other side of the planet (China, India, etc.). The laws of physics tell us that this lopsided weight distribution has created a planetary wobble that is responsible for our weather anomalies. American scientists are now realizing that this population overload on the other side of the planet may be the real cause of global warming.

[*The above nonsense is an example of how idiotic conspiracy theories get started, served up by yours truly.*]

> " A logical argument based on a faulty premise will be just as convincing as one based on a viable one. "

(Flashback Vol. 1)
A conspiracy theory thrives and derails where ignorance prevails.

COSMIC

The Alien Federation of Planets

Alien council: Now that you have returned from your scouting mission to planet Earth, what's the best thing about that world?

Alien scout: The best thing about that world is its people.

Alien council: What's the worst thing about that world?

Alien scout: The worst thing about that world is its people.

1. All of creation is antithetical. It is simultaneously beautiful and ugly, peaceful and turbulent, creative and destructive, orderly and chaotic, predictable and erratic, deadly and benign. Where do all these contradictions come from? Do you ever wonder if the gods are antithetical?

2. **The human lotto:** The difference between the existence and non-existence of planet Earth, of you being born or unborn, is based on trillions upon trillions of fortuitous events playing out exactly as they did, scattered throughout eons of time dating back to the Big Bang. Don't try to tell me you're not unique.

3. Life is a bodily journey between two unknowables.

4. **James Webb telescope:** Humanity's dark side is always on display. Nevertheless, one cannot deny the unmatched and unprecedented beauty of the human animal—distinct from all other animals in its capacity for science, not to mention its expression in literature, art, music, and philosophy. We are a flowering enigma without comparison on planet Earth. But as you know, from a cosmic perspective, that's a very narrow lens.

5. When it comes to the question of the cosmos, there can be only two possibilities: Who did it, or what did it?

6. **The unanswerable:** What is the importance of our species on planet Earth when measured against three trillion galaxies, countless stars and planets, not to mention the *billions* of pre-Earth and post-Earth years? Will there be anything left of what we consider important after our solar system is gone? In the overall scheme of things, do we have importance, or the illusion of importance? Perhaps what we really have—for our peace of mind—is the importance of illusion.

7. The question is often asked "Are we alone in the universe?" We now know that our star (sun) sits on the outer side of our 400-billion-star galaxy, awash in space with three trillion other galaxies. We may be nothing more than a grain of sand on the cosmic beach. However, there is no doubt in my mind that we are unique. But being unique does not mean we are alone.

8. **Climate change:** Is humanity our planet's weakest link, or its greatest asset? Vegas has us at even odds.

9. **Spinning our wheels:** Trying to make sense out of what we call the universe ("creation") gets harder with the acquisition of knowledge. The more we know, the less we understand. For example, the concept of God as Creator really doesn't make any sense if you study that proposition carefully. And yet, the universe without some form of ultimate Consciousness is equally senseless. Maybe our problem is that we're trying to make sense out of something that makes no sense. Is it possible that the universe is nothing more than the outcome of fortuitous randomness? We've all contemplated that possibility. But seriously, that doesn't make any sense either. Hmm . . .

> When it comes to the question of the cosmos, there can be only two possibilities: Who did it, or what did it?

10. Everything is ephemeral (fleeting, impermanent). I can't think of anything that isn't transitory. That includes all life

forms, planets, stars, galaxies, and the entire universe. Of course, religion would exempt the gods and believers from this nihilistic black hole. But is there any other way to escape this foreboding vanishing act?

(*See also Mystery/Enigma*)

(Flashback Vol. 1)

Cosmic arrogance: Just because we're a grain of sand on the cosmic beach doesn't mean we are the beach.

CULTURE AND SOCIETY

Types

It is certain that life can be chancing.
There are troublesome woes that persist.
But somewhere the people are dancing,
and doing the rock and roll twist.

There is love in the heart that is giving,
and the happy-go-lucky get kissed.
But the sluggards and slackers get angry,
making trouble and raising their fists.

I'll be clear with the words I am saying,
that despite all the griefs that exist,
we will dance while the music is playing,
and ignore all the wrongs that persist.

1. Cultural submersion blinds the eye of our judgment. How else can we explain the roaring crowd in the Roman Coliseum when human beings were slaughtered for entertainment, or the "Strange Fruit" hanging from Southern trees

prior to Civil Rights? As for today, what are the customs that blind the eye of *our* judgment?

2. Pick any social issue and you'll see that people are the problem . . . but they're also the solution.

3. **The First-World advantage:** We have many fortunes despite our misfortunes.

4. **Location, location, location:** In dictatorial countries, life has *usually* been a vale of sadness, sprinkled with brief episodes of happiness. In democratic countries, life has *usually* been a vale of happiness, sprinkled with brief episodes of sadness.

5. I've often wondered about *Star Trek's* Prime Directive—the Starfleet policy that prohibits its members from interfering with the natural development of any alien civilization they might encounter. It protected underdeveloped alien cultures from having their evolutionary process disrupted. Noble and ethical, for sure. But where would we be today if Columbus, de Soto, Cortés, and other conquistadores had labored under that same directive when they confronted the New World? Of course, the subjugation and obliteration of indigenous civilizations that occurred when they arrived is not something to be proud of. And so, we contemplate the conundrum once more: *We find the atrocities of the past to be unequivocally wicked. And yet, without that wickedness, our timeline would not exist, and neither would we.* Of course, I know that there are a multiplicity

of factors that led to our personal existence. As a wise woman once told me, "Anything and everything changes everything." However, I focused on "wickedness" because it's the one thing we wish didn't happen, without taking seriously the consequences of its absence.

6. Sometimes you hear people say that they pulled themselves up by the bootstraps, as if to imply they are self-made. However, they shouldn't forget that someone provided those boots, not to mention the straps to boot.

7. We lost over 3000 Americans when terrorists attacked the New York City Twin Towers in 2001. Because of that tragedy, hundreds of new laws and restrictions have been passed to guard against terrorists. But since that time, according to a CNN report (9-05-2022), we have lost 660,000 men, women, and children to gun violence. *660,000!!!* Just like I waited and waited for our society to finally ban smoking in public places, I find myself waiting once again for the obvious.

8. **Internet log ins:** "I am not a robot." Hmm . . . . take a class in cultural anthropology and you'll have to think twice about that one.

9. **Socially Incorrect:**

Child: Mommy Mommy, why is Daddy running across the field?

Mommy: Shut up and reload!

Child: Mommy Mommy, where did Grandpa go?

Mommy: Shut up and eat your stew!

Those old Mommy Mommy jokes that I remember from my teenage years in the 1950s don't get a pass anymore. (I could showcase some truly offensive racial jokes of that time, but I prefer not to resurrect them.) It seems that every generation adopts concepts, customs, and behaviors that are criticized and corrected by future generations. Of course, some customs are blatantly depraved. The social environments of the past that we abhor (e.g., Roman gladiators, Church-sanctioned witch-hunts, slavery, Nazism), and wonder how people justi-fied them, should serve as a clarion call for self-evaluation. Be they extreme or just bad taste, what's under our noses?

10. **The totalitarian motto:** Beat the people into submission and get rid of the ones that will not yield. (I am hopeful that in the future someone will read this and not know what it means.)

11. **The power of positive doing:** Doctors and scientists had proclaimed that breaking the four-minute mile was unat-tainable (known as the four-minute barrier). That belief lasted for decades. But in 1954, Roger Bannister shattered that myth with a record run of 3:59. However, Bannister's track record lasted just 46 days. It's the visual and the mental that facilitates. As of April 2021, the "four-minute barrier" has been broken by 1,663 athletes. This is the inverse of E

pluribus unum (Latin for "Out of many, one"), that is, out of one, many.

12. It is true that most white-collar or blue-collar workers are good at what they do. However, finding the best out of the good isn't easy. We need to remember that a deck of cards only has four aces.

> Pick any social issue and you'll see
> that people are the problem . . .
> but they're also the solution.

13. I am a *racist* because of cultural indoctrination. I am an *antiracist* because of education. I am a *nonracist* because of personal interaction.

14. **The USA vs. worldly mayhem:** We often fail to appreciate the luxury of spending a boring evening at home.

15. **The homeless:** When we were kids at the playground, we'd climb up the ladder and glide down the slide onto welcoming sand—whee! I think that's a good metaphor for life's

journey in America. Nevertheless, it is a statistical fact that some of us—without blame—will come down that slide headfirst onto nothing but concrete (lest we forget).

16. When you think about it, we are all casualties and/or beneficiaries of circumstance. Although it's not a guarantee, Americanism favors the latter. Count your blessings.

17. **The lesser of two evils (2023):** According to the CDC, gun violence overall in 2021 took the lives of 49,000 people (134 per day). However, about 54% of those were gun suicides. In comparison, according to MSNBC and other sources, in 2022, there were 71,000 drug overdose deaths (195 per day). But only 5 to 7% of those were drug suicides. At first glance, it may appear that gun violence is the lesser of two evils since death rates are lower than drug overdoses. However, we must remember that almost all overdose deaths are self-inflicted, while almost 50% of gun deaths are homicides.

18. Most people never escape from the internment camp of cultural indoctrination.

19. Civilization is the safety zone that curtails the animal aspect of our nature. It controls our wanton desires and provides for the evolving betterment of the animal within our personal aspirations. Of course, this assumes a democratic, compassionate, educated, ethical, rational, and law-abiding society. Whew!

20. **Homeless blues**: As Dorothy so rightly stated: "There's no place like home." Unfortunately, for many Americans, there's no place called home.

> " Amid worldly turmoil, most of those who reside in first-world countries take the good life for granted and fail to appreciate even the humdrum moments of their good fortune. "

21. **A Goldilocks life span**: In September of 1939, Hitler invaded Poland and started WWII. I was born that same month on American soil—into a bubble of love and middle-class prosperity. I missed WWII, the Korean War, the Vietnam War, the Iraq War, and the Afghan War for reasons of geography, age, and academic pursuit. For the past eight decades I have lived my life in a bubble of love and prosperity. Unless there is some unforeseen circumstance, this fortuitous experience will continue until I die. Over the past millenniums, how many people could have made that Goldilocks

claim? Over the next millenniums, how many people will be able to make that same claim?

22. **2025**: Criminal behavior, criminal law, nationalism, ageism, racism, misogyny, religion, and political partisanship have conflated into a heretofore unimagined national nightmare.

> Most people never escape
> from the internment camp
> of cultural indoctrination.

23. Amid worldly turmoil, most of those who reside in first-world countries take the good life for granted and fail to appreciate even the humdrum moments of their good fortune.

24. Tribalistic xenophobia and corporate greed may not be the root of all evil, but they certainly are some of the frontrunners.

25. Who are the happiest people in America? National studies continue to confirm that it's the middle class, and they are

easy to spot. They're the ones constantly trying to climb out of the middle class by winning the lotto. Go figure.

26. The world would be a much better place if people could see it from my perspective, and even more so if I could see it from theirs.

27. Books are becoming the symbolic tombstones of America's literary graveyard.

28. **2025**: Mental health is no more of a problem in the USA than anywhere else in the world. And yet, mass shootings, and gun violence in general, greatly exceed all other developed countries. The solution for reducing gun violence is gun control. I refuse to use the euphemism gun "safety." It's gun *control*, period. America has 4% of the world's population, and 50% of its guns. You can raise the issue of mental health and red flag laws all you want, but they alone will not resolve gun violence without at least four basic pragmatic gun control laws: (1) Ban assault weapons; AR-15s, AK-47s; all weapons of war, should be off limits to the public, (2) no civilian under the age of 21 should be sold a gun, (3) background checks are a must without exception, including buyers at gun shows, and (4) anyone helping someone to circumvent these regulations should be held accountable as an accessory to the crime.

29. **Perennial purification**: Yesterday's beliefs and customs were thought to be optimal, but evolving knowledge reshaped that assumption. In like manner, today's beliefs and customs

are thought to be undeniable, but tomorrow's enlightenment will modify them accordingly. Nevertheless, the beliefs and customs of our time, even when flawed, are essential aspects for personal and social stability.

(Flashback Vol. 1)
Anarchy is the end result of a society lacking civility and manifesting a disregard for the rule of law.

DEATH AND AFTERLIFE

Who Knows Where the Time Goes?

The hands of time sweep us along,
In the blink of an eye, and then we're gone.
We still have time to dance the jive,
To live and laugh while still alive.

The hands of time we can't control,
Don't live as if you're on parole.
And even if we've aged a bit,
The rule of thumb is not to sit.
Let's jump and play before we pass,
Before we lie beneath the grass.

1. **I tawt I taw a puddy tat:** In my younger day I could speed across the plain like a gazelle. That no longer seems to be the case—and the big cat behind me is in full stride closing fast.

2. Why is it that empathy, wisdom, and kindness accelerate as our life force decelerates?

3. **Arrival and departure:** Although we are thrust into this world abruptly, most of us arrive amid jubilant fanfare. We are gently cradled with caring tenderness, showered with hugs and kisses, and greeted with enthusiastic joy. Thereafter, we are helped by loved ones to take our beginning steps in a new and unfamiliar environment. Wouldn't it be wonderful if when we depart this life, we encounter that same reception? Greeted, as it were, with caring tenderness, showered with hugs and kisses, met with enthusiastic joy, and helped by loved ones to take our beginning steps in a new and unfamiliar environment.

4. If we fully understood the *improbability* of our present life, we would be more likely to entertain the *possibility* of an afterlife.

5. Death is not total extinction. It is the gateway to an energy transformation. But does this transformation come with, or without, self-awareness. Without self-awareness there is no "Somewhere Over The Rainbow." Judy and I are hoping for a multicolored afterlife.

6. What can we share with each other about the afterlife, assuming there is one? Not a thing. It would be like a bottom fish in the depths of the ocean floor telling another bottom fish what's on the other side of the water.

7. If there is an afterlife, I ask only for three things: (1) to see friends and loved ones, (2) to get the full lowdown on what this universe is all about, and (3) the absence of suffering for everyone.

8. **A candle metaphor**: When we are conceived in our mother's womb, the wick is lit. No matter the size, shape, color, or scent, the candle of life will dwindle down to its final leftover residue. The extinguished wick will remain as a crowning testimony to our absent light. Despite the ensuing darkness, I have high hopes for an afterglow.

> I define death as the absence of self-awareness.

9. The best that can happen to us when we die is to wake-up dead.

10. Life is the bullseye that death searches out. It is the unmatched random hunter. Its weapons and methods are boundless, and usually without mercy. Death can strike without warning or initiate prolonged suffering. It plays no

favorites and pulls no punches. Outer space is not the most challenging frontier to be managed. Death is.

11. **Coming and going**: No ticket into this life gives you a free ride, and the price of admission varies considerably . . . as it does with the exit portal.

12. If a person has no malice, is unbiased, and without worry, I can only conclude that they're dead.

13. Almost all the billions of people—young and old—who were alive 100 years ago are gone, and the 8 billion men, women, and children living today will mostly be gone within 100 years (barring scientific breakthroughs). That's a horrendous loss of life in a very short time. This massive turnover is ongoing and not contemplated by most. This oversight occurs because we live our lives within personal bubbles of human interaction, we live in the moment, and because the masses are wiped out by attrition. Attrition is the slow-moving process by which the Grim Reaper dulls our senses to this calamitous extermination.

14. Sooner or later everyone realizes that life isn't fair. Aside from faith-based assumptions, why do we assume that the afterlife is?

15. A *dead zone* (water without oxygen) can occur anywhere from the deep sea to smaller bodies of water. When oxygen levels drop—caused by warmer temperatures—animal and plant life slowly die off. The fish can escape, but crustaceans

aren't that lucky. The zone eventually becomes a deep-sea graveyard. As a metaphor, one can compare ocean dead zones to the human heart. When love levels drop—caused by the absence of human intimacy—the heart slowly hardens and eventually becomes a dead zone.

16. What is our definition of death? Science says our bodies don't devolve into nothing; they just break down into their constituent parts and are then recycled into the ecosystem. Whether or not we have a soul is another issue altogether. Whatever the case, I define death as the absence of self-awareness.

17. I want neither a funeral nor memorial service since I won't be able to return the favor.

18. It would be nice if death were like the tornado that whisked Dorothy and Toto away to the playful land of Oz. The added company of family and friends, some animals, and the elimination of bad witches would make it ideal. Is that too much to ask?

19. **Universal**: He who has everything has *everything to lose*. He who has nothing has *everything to lose*. It's called the breath of life.

20. **Afterlife contemplations**: The question remains: Is hope better than no hope, or is no hope better than hope? Some people are bipolar—I'm bi-hopeful.

21. **The final exit**: Long lines at the supermarket can be exasperating, especially if the cashier is lackadaisical. As an older person, I am now in the check-out line at the market of Kick the Bucket. There's only a few people left in front of me. But this is one time I hope the cashier is a slowpoke.

22. This one puzzles me: Aside from joyous reunions, what would be the purpose of eternal life? Whether or not one agrees, Mormons are the front runners on this one.

23. **The circle of life**: See it! Want it! Got it! Lost it!

24. My belief in the afterlife is not without doubt. Nevertheless, my hope leans in that direction. That certainly is the foundational reflection of all religions. Interpreted from that perspective, one of my favorite songs comes from that classic movie *The Poseidon Adventure* and is called "The Morning After" by Maureen McGovern. *(Search YouTube)*

(Flashback Vol. 1)
Incremental deterioration of the mind and body is a form of suffering dispensed throughout the aging process. For the majority of elders, death by attrition is indeed the quintessential death of a thousand cuts. But perhaps the real tragedy in life must rest with those people—some of them children—who never live long enough to experience dying in slow motion. We don't get to choose, but I prefer the former. I just wish euthanasia were an option for us elders in the event of a catastrophic ending. How long does it take for a society to come to its senses?

ELDERLY

I'm 84 In 2024

The new year starts with twenty-four.
That surely rhymes with eighty-four.
But how and why did I get this old?
A luck of the draw as I've been told.

Now looking back I will confess,
I've had my share of prime success.
But some had more, and some had less
And that's the way of life, I guess.

I fought the fight and met the test.
And found my footing in the quest.
I plumbed some oysters from the deep
And found some pearls that I could keep.

My aging number eighty-four,
Tells me I need to stay ashore.
I'm neither rich nor am I poor.

I do not want for something more.
Except, of course, to stay alive.
God help me get to eighty-five.

1. One of the benefits of reaching the age of 80 is that you don't have to have any more colonoscopies. However, one is subjected to an increasing number of doctors, X-rays, CT scans, blood draws, IVs, MRIs, and pills galore. Even so, I find this to be a most fortunate predicament.

2. Is there a significant difference between a sell-by date and an expiration date? . . . there is if you're old.

3. **Endings:** I was able to reconnect with an elderly professor of mine who was now in his 90s. He had always been a successful, flamboyant, charismatic educator and minister but was now quietly ending his life in an upscale rest home. "How are you?" I inquired. In a subdued voice, he described his present-day existence as the "emptiness of emptiness." I don't think he was being pessimistic. I think he was just acknowledging reality—the absence of the past, the infirmity of the present, and the annihilation of future promise (at least in this life).

4. I was on the phone with a friend who asked me what I was planning to do this afternoon. I replied, half seriously, that I would try to do today what I had planned to do tomorrow that I should have done yesterday.

5. Believe it or not, when I crossed into my 80s, I finally left "senior moments" behind. I am now grappling with senior minutes.

6. In most cases, we know that if we take care of our bodies, they'll take care of us. But if my inner parts look like my outer parts, I'm in real trouble.

> "
> Is there a significant difference between a sell-by date and an expiration date? . . . there is if you're old.
> "

7. I really don't like the idea of old age; there's not much future in it.

8. Knowing is a good thing. Understanding what you know is even better. That's one of the side benefits of aging. If you're missing hindsight, you lack comprehension; it's not easy to have one without the other.

9. As I continue to age, it's getting harder to know if I'm still live ammo, or a spent bullet.

10. Aside from any age-related illnesses, good brains are for-ever, while good looks are short-lived. Good luck if you have neither.

> "In most cases, we know that if we take care of our bodies, they'll take care of us. But if my inner parts look like my outer parts, I'm in real trouble. "

11. **The curse:** The other day I heard an elderly person say that getting old was a curse. I'm 84, so I think I can speak to that sentiment. The process of aging is not an easy one, and the trauma differs for everyone (especially if mental or physi-cal affliction ensues). We elders know that very few grains of sand remain in the hourglass, and incremental deterioration is a constant reminder of the inevitable slide into the abyss. Not fun. However, if one is to be honest, the curse is not get-ting old . . . the curse is not to get old.

12. Retirement is not an excuse to become useless. The way to avoid a dull and monotonous future is to maintain a useful present.

13. Sometimes elderly people looking back on their glory days can see that the glory in those days was specific to their outlook, and of little significance to others.

14. You'll never be alone, no matter how old you get; there'll always be someone around to pick your pocket.

15. One of the lessons we learn on the path to aging is that we can't know what it means to have cancer, Alzheimer's, or ALS, until we do. We can't know what it feels like to lose a child, a mother, a father, a brother, a sister, a partner, a friend, until we do. Point: *The augmentation of empathy is commensurate with advancing age.*

16. The aging process places locks on the doors of opportunity—except for the door with the exit sign.

17. The phrase "senior moment" is really a euphemism for MCI (mild cognitive impairment). However, for many seniors, wisdom and experience far outweigh the loss.

18. **Time flies:** We think of aging in one-year intervals. However, when my birthday comes around, I always think of it in two-year intervals. The day before my birthday, I go through a sobering ritual. Try it out: Let's say you're 68 and it's one day before your birthday. What does that mean? It means

that even if you're 68 in the moment, one day and one year later, you'll be 70. It's kind of unsettling when you do this even though you understand the sequencing.

19. There was a word I couldn't think of this morning, but I finally did. Now this afternoon . . . I can't think of the word I couldn't think of this morning.

20. **The heavy head syndrome:** Although our powers of recall decline as we grow older, I have also discovered that the head gets heavier and heavier with age. Mine certainly has. That's due to the many words that keep piling up on the tip of my tongue.

21. **Life's garden:** I recently turned 85. Today I am planting seeds and pulling up weeds; tomorrow I'll be pushing up daisies.

22. Given the natural incremental deterioration of the human body as the years gather, we discover that exercise is a losing battle, but a critical one, nonetheless. If you don't get after it—you will prematurely get afterlife.

23. As people advance in age, they tend to become cynical. However, if you are a cynic, we do have some remedies for this debilitating condition. A torrid romance, ice cream, chocolates, domesticated pets, family and friends, sit-coms and, more importantly, getting rid of most social media platforms, will help.

24. Despite some serious side effects, including a one-way ticket to Palookaville, growing old is a privilege.

25. I saw these words in an Internet cartoon: "Y'all enjoy those 20s, 30s, and 40s, because in your 50s, that check engine light [is] gonna come on." True enough. However, that witticism needs the following amendment: When you're in your 80s, that *fuel light* is gonna come on, and there'll be no way to refill the tank, or recharge the battery. But you'll be thankful that the car is still running.

26. **Good news, bad news:** The good news is that at the age of 85 I'm still running on all cylinders. The bad news is that my spark plugs aren't firing properly, and there's no way to replace them. But I'm grateful to still be on the road.

> You'll never be alone, no matter how old you get; there'll always be someone around to pick your pocket.

27. As I advance into my 80s, I can feel the energy of life slowly ebbing away. So be it. However, I will continue my life-long adventure any which way I can.

(Flashback Vol. 1)
I'm not afraid of dying; I'm just afraid of not living longer.

ETHICS & MORALITY

The Fire

I can see my house is burning
through the smoke and through the haze.
And I still don't know the reason
why I set my house ablaze.

Now the story I am telling
it is true and quite compelling.
With a match I really blew it,
and there's no way to undo it.

If it wasn't for my family
I'd be really in a fix.
But they made me an exception
'cause my age was only six.

1. It is better for your character to outweigh your good reputation, rather than vice versa.

2. A senior citizen's wrongdoing is a youthful indiscretion to the 10th power. Whatever your age, indiscretion is a matter of degree, not a matter of absence.

3. The occurrence of one's derogatory comments about another is usually in direct proportion to the nobility of one's character.

4. **The gray area:** People often say, "Two wrongs don't make a right." I'm not sure that's a fair assessment because it implies that there is equivalence between the two wrongs. Perhaps a minor wrong to correct a major wrong is the lesser of two evils, thereby making the minor wrong a right after all.

> The occurrence of one's derogatory comments about another is usually in direct proportion to the nobility of one's character.

5. **Situation ethics:** There are times when our moral compass should be ignored if, in fact, the moral code undermines the ultimate good.

6. The needs of the self outweigh the needs of the many, at least in one's own mind.

7. **Titanic:** I think most men want to believe they're gallant, even if they're not. However, one cannot camouflage in a crisis. In critical moments, all pretenders and their opposites are exposed. If put to the test, I'm not sure in which category I would fall.

8. It's best not to live at the top of your voice, or at the bottom of your morality.

9. **For group discussion:** Up until the end of the 1950s, high school girls that were considered promiscuous were ostracized from their peers. That norm started to change when the sexual revolution gained momentum in the '60s. Consequently, the negative stigma of that virginal loss is less relevant in the twenty-first century. This is not to imply that all high school girls today are promiscuous or are in lockstep with these permissive mores. Regardless, five questions arise: (1) Did the virtuous girls of the '50s miss out prior to the sexual sea change of the '60s, while the so-called bad girls of the '50s were judged unfairly? (2) Are cultural morals everchanging, depending on the timeline in which they exist, as seen in our previous example? (3) Are there any unchanging or universal morals? (4) If so, what is the difference between cultural morals and universal morals (if any)? (5) Finally, why was it only the girls who were judged by their behavior and not also the boys?

10. There's never a straight line between moral upbringing and immoral behavior.

11. **Seriously disingenuous:** To be untruthful for the sake of another, at the expense of one's own integrity, makes for a difficult decision.

12. There are times when the unseen sins of omission have greater consequences than those of commission. But it is only the discovered perpetrators of wrongdoing that incur retribution, while many perpetrators of omission slip away with impunity.

13. **Right and wrong:** Humans are like batteries with both negative and positive charges. However, unlike batteries, the human positive and negative aspects overlap, and they do so without equivalency.

> Can anything constructive come out of a negative comment that I make about someone else? That's the question I always ask myself before criticizing anyone.

> To be untruthful for the sake
> of another, at the expense
> of one's own integrity, makes
> for a difficult decision.

14. I don't remember hating anyone. I don't even know if I can. I do on occasion get mad and dislike someone. But that's a different animal. It probably takes a special environment or experience to create that toxic emotion. Perhaps the inability to hate is the good side effect of having lived a sheltered life.

15. **Thumper revisited**: Can anything constructive come out of a negative comment that I make about someone else? That's the question I always ask myself before criticizing anyone. If the answer is no, I keep my mouth shut.

16. **Paleontology**: According to the fossil record, our primitive ancestors had a 400cc brain. That's the brain size of a modern chimpanzee. Today, as our evolution continues, our brains measure around 1300cc. Interestingly, chimps and humans share almost 99% of their DNA. Scientists have also shown that humans share variations of DNA with other animals, even insects. Although these animals have not had the

same evolutionary trajectory that we have enjoyed, it seems that the animals we eat and hunt have *strong similarities* to the animals we once were and still are in some respects. What are the moral implications of that biological connection?

17. It is obvious that man's moral compass can sometimes go awry. That continues to be an unresolved embarrassment for the gods.

18. 'Tis better to move at a snail's pace in the right direction, than at lightning speed in the wrong direction. Of course, it's better not to move at any speed in the wrong direction.

(Flashbacks Vol. 1)
To be *self-righteous* is to wallow in the delusion of moral superiority. To be *unrighteous* is to burden oneself with unforeseen consequences. To be *righteous* is trying to be neither.

In Plato's Republic, Book II, we have the Ring of Gyges. In summary, the story is about a mysterious ring that can make you invisible when turned around on your finger. The ring, and its power to make you invisible, is used as a metaphor to expose man's true nature. In other words, if you owned such a ring, could you keep from misusing this unchecked power of invisibility? Are we inclined to be just or unjust, moral or immoral, good or evil? As for me, if I had such a ring when I was in high school, I would have made a quick trip over to the girls' gym.

FAITH/BELIEF

Cause and Effect

Of all the gods that come and go
In temples of faith where everyone goes,
We seek and request, but we don't know
If God or chance has made it so.

But chance is cold and somewhat dark
We need an arc that forms a spark.
It's faith alone that helps us cope.
And faith alone that gives us hope.

1. **Lockstep:** Most beliefs are based on consensus rather than logic or critical examination. The old saying remains relevant: "That which is popular is seldom true; that which is true is seldom popular."

2. People do not choose their beliefs; the beliefs of their time and place choose them. Translation: People have access only to the beliefs and concepts that exist within their time frame.

And the historical record tells us that most of those beliefs are time sensitive. But too often, subsequent devotees ignore their sell-by date.

3. *It's a Wonderful Life* is one of my favorite Jimmy Stewart movies, and let's not forget *Miracle on 34th Street* with Maureen O'Hara, John Payne, Edmund Gwenn, and Natalie Wood. Hollywood produces many feel-good films with Shakespeare's overriding theme that the world is more than we know. Sometimes golden nuggets of mystical vibes reverberate from the silver screen. I get goose bumps and teary-eyed when I see some of Hollywood's cinematic fantasy endings.

4. As I contemplate the afterlife, I have concluded that *hope* makes more sense to me than *faith*. Faith requires a level of complete confidence that something is true. Hope is a feeling that something desired will happen, but not considered a guarantee. I have hope, not faith. To each his own.

5. Sometimes religious faith is the outcome of naiveté. Ironically, the same can be said about the faithless.

6. The Earth's longevity—billions of years—is but a blink of an eye in the universal timeline. That's an inescapable reality. Most humans live out their lives without realizing or contemplating the impact that might have on beliefs.

7. **Stonehenge 3100 BC – 1600 BC:** For most people, beliefs are determined by the time capsule in which they are born,

along with the herd mentality of their peers. "What's in your wallet?"

8. It's hard to think we're not right on every subject. So, anyone who disagrees with us must be wrong. Rationally, we know that can't always be true. And yet, it's almost impossible for us to think otherwise. That's because we are wedded to what we believe; if we didn't believe what we believe, we would believe something else.

> "
> Faith requires a level of complete confidence that something is true. Hope is a feeling that something desired will happen, but not considered a guarantee.
> "

9. **Life's journey**: It's impossible for religious faith to remain static. It's a bit like those ever-changing transition lenses; it all depends on where you are.

10. **Goodbye Santa and the like**: As we grew older, there was a certain amount of regret in leaving behind the bulk of our childhood beliefs. Those magical concepts were filled with doubtless wonder, and disbelief was unimaginable.

11. When we seek *absolute certainty* about the gods, sacred books, or the afterlife, the attempt proves futile. However, lacking certainty should not be construed as lacking assurance. Faith is based on spiritual apprehension rather than proof.

12. **Matters beyond our control:** Here is a common expression of faith: "There but for the grace of God go I." The remark is meant to be one of thanks and gratitude. However, it seems to imply that the lucky have found favor with God, and the unlucky have not. That doesn't make sense. Is it possible that the unfortunate are simply victims of circumstance, while those with good fortune are beneficiaries of circumstance?

(Flashback Vol. 1)
I like the words from Kahlil Gibran's masterpiece, *The Prophet*: "And if you would know God be not therefore a solver of riddles. Rather look about you and you shall see Him playing with your children. And look into space; you shall see Him walking in the clouds, outstretching His arms in the lightning and descending in rain. You shall see Him smiling in flowers, then rising and waving His hands in the trees."

FAME AND FORTUNE

The Phil Spector Syndrome

(This poem from Vo1 1)

Failure hurts
and it hurts very deeply.
But fame has the potential
to destroy completely.

1. **The never-ending parade**: Each new generation is always on the hunt for fresh blood. As an example, hardly any of my college students ever heard of Ricky Nelson. Lost in the shadows of a bygone era, this mega star spent most of his childhood on TV and became a teen idol while placing 53 songs on the *Billboard Hot 100* between 1957 and 1973. Bottom line: Almost all of us shrivel up and fade away. To rephrase an old saying: The wheels of *time* grind slowly, but they grind exceedingly fine.

2. **Beatlemania and Taylor Swift**: Acknowledging and appreciating creative talent showcased on the playing field of life is

a good thing. But anyone who makes an idol of the gifted is the hallmark of someone yet to come of age.

3. The best or the worst thing that can happen to anyone is when the fantasy dream becomes reality.

4. I'd rather be a small fish in a big pond, than a big fish in a small pond. The former allows plenty of others to swim free; the latter sucks all the oxygen out of the water.

5. **Ephemeral**: The flame of fame, whatever the sort, whatever the length of time, is mostly relegated to the dustbin of history by the slow-burning candle of impermanence.

6. Do you know what it feels like to be so famous and charismatic that when you walk into a room full of strangers, everyone there is eclipsed? It's an amazing experience of which I know nothing about.

7. The Beach Boys without Brian fancy themselves to be creative, and to some extent they are. But much of what they have accomplished they owe to the one who paved the way. After all, adding the caboose to a train already standing is the easiest part of being creative. I too take that lesson to heart.

8. **Ambition**: Whether the outcome be success or failure, don't reach for the big enchilada unless you have the stomach for it.

> " The best or the worst thing that can happen to anyone is when the fantasy dream becomes reality. "

9. I don't envy people with celebrity status. With few exceptions, climbing down from the pinnacle of success is an arduous journey, and the difficulty of that downward spiral is commensurate with the height of their stardom.

10. **Kudos to filmmaker/actor Michael Landon:** I never watched *Little House on the Prairie* without a box of Kleenex nearby.

11. **May the Force be with you:** We experience *genuine* joy through acts of kindness, not through the acquisition of fame, power, and wealth. However, the acquisition of fame, power, and wealth can help to increase those acts of kindness, *if we so choose.*

12. We all had childhood dreams. However, we could not become what we were never capable of becoming, regardless of *The Little Engine That Could*.

13. **Alone in a crowd:** Sometimes I feel sorry for POTUS, the FGK (field goal kicker), or anyone else where the buck stops. Of course, on a minor scale, the buck stops with each of us in one way or another. But a do-or-die scenario played out on the national stage is another thing altogether.

14. What is worse in the social order—being a has-been or a never-was? They both have their advantages.

15. **He who hesitates forgoes:** No matter who you are, or where you are, the door of opportunity seldom opens. The *key* to success is knocking hard. (Was that a pun?)

> We experience genuine joy through acts of kindness, not through the acquisition of fame, power, and wealth. However, the acquisition of fame, power, and wealth can help to increase those acts of kindness, if we so choose.

> "
> What is worse in the social order—
> being a has-been or a never-was?
> They both have their advantages.
> "

16. **A recipe for success:** (1) A pinch of talent. (2) Add a great deal of perseverance. (3) Mix those in with a heck of a lot of luck. BINGO!

17. Some people are born too soon or start too late. Some people are born too late or start too soon. But for those who are truly gifted—and there aren't many—it usually doesn't matter when they're born or when they start, assuming of course they have ambition and a modicum of luck.

18. It's been said that it's better to have been a "has been" than a "never was." However, the inverse of that belief may carry more weight. Many celebrities tell us that coming down from the summit is painfully agonizing; that's a bullet dodged by non-celebs.

19. **In the driver's seat:** Once you're on top and in the fast lane, never presume you can bypass everyone else in front of

you by crossing over those double yellow lines—too much vanity leads to a head-on collision.

20. Life's experiences and outcomes are based not only on the decisions we make, but also on our lifetime of might-have-beens, and equally so on the "ifs" of others.

(Flashback Vol. 1)
We seldom get to be first chair in the orchestra of life. But I'd rather play second fiddle than to play no fiddle at all.

FAMILY & FRIENDS

(This paragraph from Vol 1)

Clouds are beautiful and always unique. We take them for granted because they're always around. But their moment in time is distinct, never to be repeated. So, gaze at them closely because you'll never see the likes of any one of them again; no one will. Similarly, our family and friends are beautiful and unique, and we often take them for granted as we do the passing clouds overhead. But what you have with family and friends you'll never have again. Just like those clouds that are one-of-a-kind, once they're gone, they're gone for good.

1. It appears that 93% of Americans believe that abortion is acceptable if the life of the mother is at risk. That's a shocking statistic! I'm not talking about the 93% . . . I'm talking about the 7%. Who are these naysayers anyway?

2. The empty space between a fledgling bird in flight and the vacant nest below is crucial. In like manner, the empty space between adolescent and parent is equally so.

3. Family is either an orchard of plenty, or a wasteland of familiarity.

4. **Growing up:** We were stretched or stunted by the people who surrounded us.

5. **Similar caliber:** We all run in circles of comfort, and the circles in which we run are usually predetermined by our limitations and strong suits. Check out your friends—most of them are not too far removed in manner. Ironically, sometimes family members are the outliers.

> If you want to know who your true friends are, write a book and see who buys it. Even better, see who reads it.

6. It's a sad family affair if the seed falls *too far* from the tree; neither the tree nor the seed can move to reconnect.

7. Wisely, a parent should not punish a child for a mistake the child has a right to make based on age—admonish, yes;

punish, no. Please take this advice with a grain of salt . . . I never raised one of my own.

8. Having kids is nothing I know about. But I've seen it from both sides of that equation. It seems that such family relationships can be utterly wonderful, or frosty and bitter, and sometimes destructive. The world is indebted to parents who love their children well.

9. If you want to know who your true friends are, write a book and see who buys it. Even better, see who reads it.

(Flashback Vol. 1)
I am overwhelmed with exuberant gratitude for being raised by a mother and family that surrounded me with whole-hearted love. I only wish it could be so for everyone.

HISTORY

Jilted

I dated a girl who was really a pearl.
She had left her old lover his name was Earl.
When I gave her the ring that I put on her finger,
She was gone in a flash not a moment to linger.
Even today she remains quite a mystery.
But I'm happy to say she is nothing but history.

1. **History:** The recording of past events in human affairs is a composition of biased and unbiased storytelling. Historical embellishment and disinformation is not a question of *if*—it's a question of *how much*.

2. Not only is history written by the winners, sometimes it's written by the last one standing.

3. **Jonestown:** Sometimes a "religious" leader is more dangerous than one who is not. But history tells us that it's usually the other way around.

4. **An Oppenheimer reprieve**: People don't realize that when our B-29s fire-bombed the city of Tokyo on the night of 9-10 March 1945, those incendiary bombs killed 100,000 Japanese civilians in a single night. It was one of the most destructive bombing raids in human history. It was at least as destructive as the atomic bomb dropped on Hiroshima in August of that same year (80,000 civilian casualties with additional radiation deaths). The Tokyo raid also killed more than twice as many civilians than those killed by the A-bomb dropped on Nagasaki. (Stats taken from Britannica & Wikipedia.)

5. History is awash with freethinkers that are buried and forgotten in the Avant-garde cemetery.

6. **Millennial losses**: Historical content is subject to spring cleaning. Every new generation must decide what to eliminate from its textbooks to keep the record manageable. It's the loss of history by way of attrition, despite the Internet factor. Throughout history, we have lost tons of valuable oral and written information no longer retrievable.

7. If one could truly focus on the sweep of history over the past five thousand years, one could easily recognize the ephemeral and shifting belief systems of all things that were at one time thought to be inalterably sacred.

8. History continues to demonstrate that reasoning from a position of ignorance or pride can lead individuals, and even nations, to catastrophic consequences.

9. **2025 Retrospect**: A myopic view of American history leaves one with the impression that we are living in unprecedented dangerous times. If by that we mean the present danger is unique, we are certainly right. However, if by that we mean the danger is greater than ever before, the jury is still out.

> " History continues to demonstrate that reasoning from a position of ignorance or pride can lead individuals, and even nations, to catastrophic consequences. "

10. **Manifest Destiny**: Do you ever wonder how advanced the American Indian would be today if the pioneers had never moved West? Would the Indians still be living in teepees today? Setting aside the immoral destruction of an indigenous culture, we could agree that Manifest Destiny was inevitable and that the outcome was for the greater good. However, that belief centers only on what has transpired, without the benefit of seeing what might have transpired.

11. **Women in Europe's Middle Ages**: When you were a child, you were afraid of the night (as most children are). When you became an adult, you were also afraid of the day. Those who know their medieval history will understand why this is so.

12. **"Que Sera, Sera"**: Most of us will not even show up as footnotes on the historical timeline. At best, we will surface only on the family tree. But according to the science of astro-biology—and the biblical Book of Revelation—neither history nor family trees will survive (albeit for different reasons).

13. **Lest we remember**: All progress and achievements come with a price. Sometimes at the expense of human life. These trailblazers should not be forgotten, but they usually are. Aside from a few historical standouts, it seems that we only care about where we are, not where we've been, and not about those who got us here.

(Flashback Vol. 1)
History teaches us that you can muscle people into compliance, but you can't muscle them out of defiance.

HUMANS

Heart

The eyes are the window to the soul
That's what they say, and it may be so.
But the heart without a radiant glow
Will tell me all I need to know.

1. We could not reach for the stars until we learned the art of reaching. It was not the gods that taught us that skill. That expertise was self-taught, and honed through the human qualities of imagination, curiosity, and ingenuity. But the question remains: How did we come by those abilities? Hmm . . .

2. **Non-equivalent:** It is easier for the human spirit to rise above misfortune than it is to rise above atrocity. And somewhere in-between is betrayal.

3. As they say, "You can put lipstick on a pig, but it's still a pig." Likewise, you can put clothes on a human, but it's still

an animal. That may be a flawed analogy, but there's a truism in there somewhere.

4. Will there ever come a time when the term "humankind" will refer primarily to disposition rather than category?

5. **"What's It All About, Alfie?"** To love and to be loved (hopefully). To get educated (if possible). To improve the human condition (that's doable). Finally, not to wait until Thanksgiving to be thankful. That's what it's all about, Alfie.

6. The enemies of man are ignorance, superstition, and base tendencies. Education and knowledge help to mitigate the first two, but base inclinations remain untamed and tend to go amuck despite civilized influences.

7. For some people, feeling bad is their way of feeling good.

8. The brain is the central computer of all things human. That's probably why nature provides more head covering to the woman. Hmm . . .

9. **A Titanic metaphor:** Some people are like icebergs— detached, afloat, on their own, cold, and with flaws submerged. So, be on the lookout they can be dangerous.

10. The only thing worse than a poor loser is a poor winner. Even so, most of us are good sports either way. However, when the stakes are high, it's never been easy to win humbly or to lose graciously.

> Will there ever come a time when the term "humankind" will refer primarily to disposition rather than category?

11. Those who do not understand the animal side of human nature understand neither animals, humans, nor nature.

12. The "lower" animals are narrowly *selective* when they kill. In contrast, humans kill anything that crawls, runs, swims or flies, including their own kind. On the other hand, no other creature is as productive, constructive, and creative as are humans. Obviously, we are one of Nature's beautiful yet enigmatic contradictions.

13. To downplay, disparage, or de-emphasize the good side of human nature is to be skewed in the wrong direction.

14. Like a boat without a rudder, or a submarine without ballast, a life without mythos lacks direction and stability.

15. **Human gravity:** I agree that we are all created equal. However, we are not equally created. That is, we are equal in terms of our inherent worth as human beings, but we are

not equal in terms of our inherent gifts. In this respect, like it or not, the mental and physical inequalities between us will surface, and selective discrimination will result. As a natural consequence, we will unconsciously gravitate to our own like-minded and like-gifted circle. Show me who you run with, and I'll show you who you are.

16. Breaking a bad habit is extremely difficult; developing one is surprisingly easy.

> " Why is the name Scrooge mainly remembered in terms of what he was, rather than what he became? This seems to be a common playbook for humans. "

17. **Dualism—it's our choice:** The shortcomings of human nature—war, greed, hate, etc.—are laid out in the chronicles of history. In contrast, the perennial good side of humanity is equally reflected in art, music, literature, altruism, and so

forth. This reminds me of the old wise woman who had one proverbial wolf on each shoulder. The wolves were constantly fighting with each other, symbolizing the dogfight between the forces of good and evil. A young lad approached the wise woman and asked which wolf she thought would win the battle. The woman replied: "The one I feed the most."

18. Every poor person, every rich person, every middle-class person, every VIP, everyone of any station, is flawed by virtue of their human nature. We all know this. We just need to keep that in mind when we put someone on a pedestal—and not be so resentful and unnerved when they fall off.

19. **A Christmas Carol:** The dictionaries define Scrooge as a miserly curmudgeon and a penny-pinching cheapskate. Why is the name Scrooge mainly remembered in terms of what he was, rather than what he became? This seems to be a common playbook for humans.

20. **The moral ledger:** We are all part of the human family. That designation comes with a lot of positives and negatives, not only collectively, but individually. However, it's the pluses and minuses of all of us combined that determines whether our species resides on the positive or negative side of that spectrum. Ponder for a moment: Assuming they could, how do you think the other animals on this planet would rate us? Seriously!

21. Tigger proclaims: "But the most wonderful thing about Tiggers is I'm the only one." That's a universal truism: We are all the only one!

22. **Losers and winners:** A loser is not about someone who loses; it's about someone who is a poor excuse of a human being. Based on that criterion, I know there are more winners than losers on this planet, even though the losers make it seem otherwise. Take heart!

23. It is obvious that we, in this finite stage, are not meant, or able, to comprehend the meaning of life and death, much less the Ultimate Mystery behind it all. Perhaps life is a desert crossing, and the visualized heavenly oasis is nothing more than a mirage. Billions of people of all faiths are betting it's real. I have some doubts, but I'm not without hope.

24. **Life's journey:** Never-ending successions of losing and winning, suffering and well-being, sadness and joy, are the balancing counterpoints that lead to personal growth, if we so choose.

25. There is no such thing as a highpoint in one's life. *Life itself is the highpoint*, if one understands the uniqueness of it. Therefore, whatever happens in life, good or bad, is simply a variation of that highpoint. I guess that's easy to say when you're not hurting.

26. **Tribalism:** The first destructive problem with tribalism is that everyone outside of the tribe gets dehumanized and

demonized. The second destructive problem with tribalism is the boomerang effect.

27. If you do something wrong and fall into a deep hole, look up to the people who can toss you a rope.

28. We must always resist and expose the foolishness and the lies of misguided, mean-spirited, abusive, and malicious people. These are the enemies that work against our most noble aspirations, put us at risk, and stymie human progress.

> It is obvious that we, in this finite stage, are not meant, or able, to comprehend the meaning of life and death, much less the Ultimate Mystery behind it all.

29. There are certain human traits and needs that we all share. This creates the impression that we are alike. Well, yes and no. Snowflakes are alike, but they're not identical (to the best of our knowledge).

30. Why are we here? Aside from taking care of each other, we are here to enjoy, secure, and innovate the present, prepare for the future, nurture our spirituality, and learn from our past. That is our assignment. That is all we need to know, and all we'll ever need to know.

31. From childhood years through our senior years, life is a series of hellos and goodbyes.

32. **Mixed metaphors:** Although we can never walk in someone else's shoes, we should never stop trying. However, to avoid painful blisters, make sure the shoes are not bigger than your feet. Translation: "Don't bite off more than you can chew."

33. **Who, me?** People will disagree, but that's not the problem. The problem is how they handle those disagreements.

(Flashback Vol. 1)
The failure to forgive is a squandered opportunity for momentous self-improvement.

HYPOCRISY

Naked Bias

(This paragraph from Vol 1)

There are 1.8 billion Muslims in the world; fewer than one percent of all Muslims are terrorists. And yet, we call this miniscule number of extremists Islamic terrorists, paying little heed to the fact that we have smeared the entire religion of Islam by association. What about us? White supremacist groups, the KKK, and lone wolves have claimed authority through biblical and Christian teachings. Why don't we call these miniscule groups Christian terrorists? Hmm . . .

1. When a con man waves hello or shakes your hand, just remember—there's a middle finger in there somewhere.

2. **Blind spot**: Recognizing our own hypocrisy, although quite visible to others, is like trying to spot germs without a microscope.

3. The devil's not in the house of the rising sun, just some naked people trying to get through life as best they can. As the New Testament declares: "Why do you see the speck in your neighbor's eye but do not notice the log in your own eye?" Admittedly, I need some eyewash. Don't we all?

> When a con man waves hello or shakes your hand, just remember—there's a middle finger in there somewhere.

4. We humans tend to be unconsciously hypocritical. It's a blind spot that carries the inability to recognize when one's moral standards or beliefs do not conform with one's behavior. Unconscious hypocrisy may be one explanation why some politicians and TV evangelists do not always practice what they preach. But then again, who does?

5. The overwhelming impulse to rationalize drives the human mind to rank hypocrisy. This self-deception is a blind spot for the individual, but it is easily spotted by an outsider.

(Flashback Vol. 1)
Getting your share: Don't worry about hypocrisy; there's more than enough to go around.

JUSTICE/JUDICIAL

Injustice

Tell me it's true or tell me it isn't
unfortunate people are sittin' in prison.
Although some are guilty as surely we know,
they have better chances with plenty of dough.
I'll tell you no secrets there's always that hitch,
it's usually the poor and it's seldom the rich.

1. **VIPs:** Anyone who says, "No one is above the law," and then turns around and says, "but this is an unusual case,"—as if to invoke an exception—contradicts and weakens American jurisprudence.

2. The difference between revenge and retribution is not easily discerned, and at times are incorrectly used synonymously. As in a tapestry, these nouns are woven together and intertwined. However, the emphasis on color and design is easy to spot. To be clear, retribution is punishment mandated by

law in the pursuit of justice, while revenge is personal punishment not legally sanctioned.

3. **Under the law**: Our legal system declares that no one is
above the law. But is Lady Justice really blindfolded when it
comes to the not-so-average defendant? The stats tell us no.
If you break it down by wealth, ethnicity and race, the blindfold metaphor becomes unconvincing. Furthermore, those
who look suspicious are more likely to be convicted, even
if they are innocent. What the accused is facing here is the
stigma of negative presence in the courtroom. And if their
attorney lacks charisma and communication skills, the ineq-
uity is amplified. We're better than we were, but we still have
a long way to go. Thankfully, the continued aspiration for the
greater good is what really makes America great.

4. The rule of law is the fortified cage that keeps the human
animal in check. An autocratic leader holds the key that
unlocks that cage. We'd better believe it.

5. It seems that people must be the victims of brutality before
they feel and understand the rage of retribution. But the
question arises: Where is the dividing line between justified
retribution and unwarranted revenge? The *rational answer* to
that question should not be made by the wounded heart.

6. **Young, midlife, elderly**: There is a definite correlation
between one's wisdom and one's age. Longevity has its
rewards, and youth has its missteps. However, sometimes the
inverse of that is true. So, does it matter if we die when we're

at our best, or when we're at our worst (regardless of age)? In other words, are we judged on who we are at the time of death, or on who we were at a more innocent age, or, assuming positive improvement, judged on what we could have been had we lived longer? Hmm . . .

> "
> Too often, the amount of
> money you have determines the
> amount of justice you receive.
> "

7. **The scales of Justice**: Although no one should be above the law, I believe the greater problem is that too many minority and underprivileged people are below the law. Too often, the amount of money you have determines the amount of justice you receive. *Equality under the law* seems more of a cliché than a reality. However, we're much better off than we were, and I believe we'll be much better off than we are—if Lady Justice is a lady after all.

8. Maybe someone should take the blindfold off Lady Justice so she can see what she's doing.

9. They tell us that no one is above the law. Theoretically, that's true. Realistically, it's not. It seems that some people are beyond the law—the privileged and the powerful.

(Flashback Vol. 1)
Social justice without religion is fine; religion without social justice is not.

KNOWLEDGE & EDUCATION

A Minister's Lament

There once was a teacher named Judy,
Who everyone thought was a beauty.
I'm sorry to say she was snooty,
And kicked me around with her bootie.

There once was a teacher named Kitty,
Who everyone thought was so pretty.
I wrote her a poem very witty,
But she turned me away, what a pity.

There once was a teacher named Janet,
Whose beauty transcended this planet.
I conjured a plan and began it,
But she finally told me to can it.

So take my advice as a preacher,
Don't ever engage with a teacher.

1. **The ornament:** Many past writers, thinkers, philosophers, historians, scientists, teachers, family members, and friends have nurtured the Christmas tree of knowledge on which I now hang my ideas.

2. **I.Q. test:** Do you know the difference between ascent/assent, imminent/eminent, squash/quash, ensure/insure, sensual/sensuous, falsies/falsities. I bet that last one caught your attention.

3. I pride myself on the knowledge I have acquired over the years. In fact, I know almost everything there is to know about very little.

4. Einstein is quoted as saying that "Imagination is more important than knowledge." Who am I to disagree with Einstein? However, his comment needs an alternative approach. I would be more inclined to say that imagination is *as* important as knowledge. Without knowledge, one's imagination is limited; without imagination, knowledge becomes stagnant. Indeed, this symbiotic relationship ensures a back-and-forth feed that leads to a greater good.

5. The only thing more irritating than the mind of a know-nothing person is the mind of a know-it-all person.

6. **The first little pig:** Looking for information consistent with one's beliefs, while ignoring information that is not, allows only for the building of straw houses—houses of half-truths

and untruths that will eventually be blown away by the winds of knowledge.

7. You just need to know only a little more than most people do to make them think you know more than you do.

> "
> I pride myself on the knowledge
> I have acquired over the years.
> In fact, I know almost everything
> there is to know about very little.
> "

8. **Higher education:** Sometimes, knowledge is painful. It can separate you from family and friends and cast you away from tribal warmth. But you can't go back.

9. **Second thoughts:** Why do people rebuke a person who changes their mind or has a change of heart? After all, well-grounded information will sharpen one's judgment, as it should. Advanced knowledge pulls us away from a past line of thought, and into an upgraded way of reasoning.

10. Many Americans are less educated than I am, and that worries me. I wonder if I worry those who are more educated than I am.

11. Most of my friends know that I am an avid fan of higher education. But that doesn't mean I view it as a panacea. Some of the whackiest people we know are highly educated. I'm simply saying that the uneducated masses are more suscep-tible to the wrongdoings of the unprincipled educated. Fur-thermore, when I speak of education, I'm talking about the liberal arts courses that educate the mind, e.g., psychology, philosophy, anthropology, sociology, logic, and so forth, as opposed to occupational education (e.g., computer program-ing, mechanics, business, engineering, etc.). Unfortunately, I fear the former is giving way to the latter. However, they need not be mutually exclusive. A two-tier educational approach would be optimum, and society would be the beneficiary.

12. Those who are uneducated are less likely to grasp the ruinous effects of an uneducated society. Those who are edu-cated are less likely to grasp the importance of those who are uneducated.

13. **Double jeopardy**: I must be wary of people who know less than I do, and likewise of those who know more. I guess all of us are simultaneously on both sides of that equation.

14. **Enhancing the learning curve**: Higher education is a must if one is to escape the indoctrinated beliefs of parental and societal influences that are not always based on logic or

critical thinking. Thereafter, one should realize that higher education may also be a means of indoctrination from which one needs to escape. And it's the escapees that continue to help evolve higher education, from which the next generation needs to escape to further the process.

15. The cataracts of social conditioning and ignorance are excised by education. To what degree depends on the education.

16. **Understanding**: Our ascending level of knowledge is in direct proportion to our reasoning capability. The continuing quest for understanding is paramount. The historical record clearly demonstrates—along with stunted cultures—that the level of knowledge achieved is the most important factor that determines our best approximation of reality.

17. **The seeker's motto**: It is better to be perplexed by the uncertainties of open-mindedness than to be unperplexed by the certainties of close-mindedness.

18.
You don't know what you don't know until you go to grammar school.

You don't know what you don't know until you go to junior high.

You don't know what you don't know until you go to senior high.

You don't know what you don't know until you go to college.

You don't know what you don't know until you get your masters.

You don't know what you don't know until you get your PhD.

Thereafter, what you know is that you don't know.

19. Just because you're not educated doesn't mean you're not wise; just because you're educated doesn't mean you are.

> " Those who are uneducated
> are less likely to grasp
> the ruinous effects of an
> uneducated society. "

20. Education is the bridge to knowledge. Knowledge is the bridge to understanding. Understanding is the bridge to thinking broadly. Thinking broadly is the bridge to tolerance. Tolerance is the bridge to acceptance. Acceptance is the key to world peace. But it all begins with education. Or . . . you could take a shortcut and run with "Love your neighbor as yourself."

21. One doesn't have to be educated to display common sense, and the fact that one is educated doesn't guarantee that one does.

22. Higher education that excludes the humanity courses—history, ethics, world religions, philosophy, logic, and so forth—could diminish a student's ability to think logically, write cogently, and ponder broadly.

23. A good education helps you to know *what not to believe*, not necessarily what to believe. However, with augmented knowledge, individuals can rationally sharpen their opinions and are less likely to embrace distorted worldviews.

24. During childhood, both negative and positive beliefs are laid out before us like a newly-paved sidewalk that quickly solidifies. In like manner, our beliefs harden and become less subject to revision or rejection. Are we not all victims of solidification? However, many of those hardened beliefs can be modified or obliterated with the jackhammer of objective knowledge, that is, information based on fact, not on personal feeling, herd mentality, or confirmation bias.

25. A strong belief in Buddhism is that *a man who does not love himself cannot love others; it is impossible.* Therefore, self-love—not to be confused with narcissism—should be viewed as a positive, not a negative. Doesn't the New Testament advocate the same? (Love your neighbor as yourself.) It seems that self-love is the prerequisite for loving others.

26. We are all ignorant of our ignorance. To be aware that one is ignorant of one's ignorance is a self-imposed blessing; it is the beginning of humility, and the mitigation of hubris.

27. **Plato's Cave:** We have moved out of the dark shadowy cave of simplicity into the light of complexity in all disciplines of human endeavor. But the cave's exit point is an illusion. We have not really left the cave. We are simply approaching the cave's entrance where the light continues to beckon. I don't believe we will ever get outside of this metaphorical cave. However, our mission is to proceed toward the entrance by continuing to light lamps against the shadows of ignorance, superstition, and disinformation.

28. I do not claim to be right on all issues. But I do claim the right of struggle—the struggle to search beyond what I've been told, sold, and taught.

29. **University sine qua non:** I believe in the humanity courses of higher education because they can help mitigate ignorance, cultural bias, and *elevate* our citizenry. They don't call it *higher* education for nothing.

30. **Oops:** I try to stay away from people who hold strong opinions with no factual or historical knowledge to back them up. But sometimes in conversation I find myself being that person that I try to stay away from.

31. **Flowers for Algernon:** A person with low motivation is like a rowboat with one oar—but that's usually a personal

choice. A person with an IQ below 70 is like a rowboat without oars—that's not a choice. In that last regard, I am hopeful that we will allow futuristic AI and genetic engineering to help solve such an unfortunate fate.

> "
> One doesn't have to be educated to display common sense, and the fact that one is educated doesn't guarantee that one does.
> "

32. I'm smarter than I think I am, but dumber than I thought I was. What?

33. **Food for thought**: It is unlikely that two people will have the same IQ; but even if two people have the same IQ, it is unlikely that they will have the same KQ (knowledge). Even if two people have the same IQ and KQ, it is unlikely that they will have the same EQ (environment/experience). But even if they have the same IQ, KQ, and EQ, it is unlikely that they will have the same flexibility of mind, or the same ability to connect the dots. Some people just can't think straight. Irrational thought is evident in both progressive and conservative camps, although not with equivalence.

34. True knowledge does not always come from the knowledge or opinions of others. For sure, what we learn from others is a starting point, but it will not suffice as ultimate knowledge. This was a lesson well learned when I went to college. For example, I had always believed that the world was very old because that's what I had been told since childhood. But a collegiate course in geology solidified that view as unquestionable. I now owned the concept based on substantial evidence—it was no longer secondhand knowledge assumed to be true. I knew now that it was true, and why it was true, based on the vetted sources I was presented. Having said that, I recognize that we cannot know everything about everything. Therefore, our knowledge must be balanced against the knowledge of others, and those sources must also be vetted.

(Flashback Vol. 1)
The only thing I know for sure is that I'm smart enough to know that I could have been a lot smarter.

LOGIC

An 1867 Ant Colony in Indian Territory

Ant #1 – We're in real trouble. We don't have enough food to feed our young.

Ant #2 – We should pray to the Ant God for assistance.

Ant #1 – That won't help. Some of our brethren have been praying for days. I'm not even sure there is an Ant God.

Ant #2 – Blasphemy! You've got to have faith!

Ant #3 – Hey everyone, I just came in from outside. We've discovered one of those giant two-legged food sources just a few feet from our entrance. It struggles against some unknown restraints but remains immobilized. It has ears, eyes, and a nose for easy pickings.

Ant #2 – It's a Miracle! Our prayers have been answered. Well #1, what say ye now about our Ant God?

Ant #1 – I don't think you have considered all the "cause and effect" possibilities.

EPILOGUE: That was the day that
Ant #1 was ostracized from the colony.

1. For some, logic has been the death knell of belief, and they have buried it in the cemetery of close-mindedness. For others, logic has been the reinterpretation of belief, and the resurrection of open-mindedness.

2. When an individual's misdeeds are exposed, lying is a natural, almost uncontrollable, instinct. It's a survival defense mechanism, and few there be that can rise above it. Therefore, when people are accused of wrongdoing, we should expect the expected. On the other hand, this anticipated denial presents an almost insurmountable predicament for the accused innocent.

3. Anyone with a modicum of wisdom will understand that confirmation bias is a matter of degree, not a matter of absence.

4. The populist Will Rogers said, "I never met a man I didn't like." That comment doesn't ring true because it implies that all men are likeable. However, a closer look at his comment negates that implication. For example, he didn't say, "I never *knew* a man I didn't like." Meeting and knowing a person are two different animals. The meeting aspect is superficial, the knowing aspect is revelatory. Bottom line: It's possible to say, "I never met a man I didn't like," but it's not believable to say that I liked every man I came to know.

5. **False Dilemma?** Are humans the ultimate jewel of God's universal creation, or one of nature's normal biological outcomes? That question may be an either-or fallacy.

6. **Statistical misdirect**: The media has made a statistical comparison between the 1400 Israelis killed by Hamas on Oct.7, and the United States population. According to the media, the tragedy of what happened in Israel would be the equivalence of 50,000 dead Americans. I believe this to be a false equivalent, or a misdirect. I will use an extreme hypothetical example to illustrate my point. Imagine, if you will, an island with only two people. The island is invaded by a terrorist who kills one of the islanders. Statistically, he has killed 50% of the population. In comparison, if you killed 50% of Americans, that would total over 150 million dead. Although the stats are technically correct, to consider those outcomes equally relevant would be ludicrous. I think it was Mark Twain who said, "There are three kinds of lies: White lies, black lies, and statistics."

> If you consider someone to be wise, consider yourself to be wise. Wisdom can only be discerned by those who have it.

7. **The fourth R**: Almost everyone knows about the three Rs (**R**eading, w**R**iting, and a**R**ithmetic). They are the basic skills

taught in schools and considered to be of utmost importance. Rightly so. Sadly, there is one basic skill missing that should be a mandatory subject prior to that high school diploma. Reasoning should be the fourth R (informal logic—the ways we recognize correct from incorrect thinking). Aside from the three Rs, I can't imagine a more powerful and positive influence for the greater good. Why basic logic isn't required boggles my mind.

8. **Cause and effect:** The will of God is often confused with man's lack of knowledge, coincidence, or the randomness of nature.

9. **Horse sense:** Nationalism is the byproduct of familiarity. We are attached to our homegrown societal racetrack, and we run the race together as indoctrinated jockeys for the common good. God bless America. However, we won't understand the common good *worldwide* until we discard the horse blinders.

10. **Pitiful me:** When tragedy strikes, wisdom and common sense transforms the "why me" bewilderment into a "why not" understanding.

11. We condemn the evil of past atrocities without realizing that it was a major contributing factor that made our lives possible in the present. That is, if A had not happened, B wouldn't have followed. Consider, for example, the mass population variations in marital and offspring possibilities that were caused by the casualties of WWI and II. Those casualties

created a multiplicity of variables that are responsible for the existence of most people living today. Had those wars not occurred, others would exist in our place. This is not to think of evil as positive, but simply to recognize the irony of it all.

12. **Stats:** If God intervenes in human affairs, as many people believe, why are negative outcomes so statistically predictable? They are consistent in all categories and apply to all individuals regardless of gender, race, ethnicity, nationality, or faith. That doesn't necessarily exclude one's belief in a personal loving God, but it may give us a better understanding of how the game of life should be played.

13. If you consider someone to be wise, consider yourself to be wise. Wisdom can only be discerned by those who have it.

14. . An elderly person is less likely to make unwise decisions than a young person. That's why the phrase "Don't trust anyone over thirty" is misleading. On the other hand, a young person is less likely to be jaded, disillusioned, or cynical by life's realities and disappointments. That's why the phrase "Don't trust anyone under thirty" is misleading. As implied, exceptions are to be noted on both sides of that equation.

15. Normally, amazement and curiosity about the everyday world escapes us. Familiarity is the culprit. Accordingly, we are amazed only by those things that rest outside of the norm; we fail to see that the common is no less astonishing than the uncommon. For example, the healer's power—or whatever it

is—that restores a crippled hand draws attention. But the act is no more miraculous than the hand itself.

16. The problem we face with the phrase "critical thinking" is that most people don't even know what is meant by critical thinking, much less practice it. Ironically, the survival of civilization has always depended on those who do, but also on those who don't. Go figure.

17. Extremists can cherry-pick the facts and then spin them beyond rational limits, albeit not recognized as misleading by the misinformed layperson. Of course, none of us consider ourselves to be misinformed.

18. The first rule of thumb when driving in the fog is to never turn on your high beams. High beams in the fog will greatly impair your vision as the light ricochets back. That's why Rudolph's bright nose never made any sense to me when Santa asked him to guide his sleigh on that foggy night. For that reason, I have concluded that Rudolph is not a true part of the Santa story.

19. The dominance of partisan passion over common sense leads to damnable behavior, be it political or religious.

(Flashback Vol. 1)
You cannot reason but from what you know, and that's why the reasoning of most people is unreasonable.

LOVE/KINDNESS

Kindness

When I think of the kings in the days of yore
With riches and shelter and foods galore,
I wonder why kings had not opened the door
To the weak and the lonely, the lost and the poor.

Yet here in the present I'm more than a king
With shelter and food and not needing a thing.
But now I must ponder if I give to the poor
With little regard as the kings of yore.

1. Religious belief or unbelief is not the significant difference between people; it's between those who are kind and those who are not.

2. We serve ourselves best when we serve others first.

3. Gloves protect the hands of a pick-and-shovel worker from getting callouses. Tender hearts have no such protection. But

even though they are prone to get stressed, often bruised, and sometimes broken, they seldom get calloused.

4. **Empathy**: If you cannot fill your eyes with tears, you cannot see clearly.

5. A person's goodness is not determined by belief, unbelief, or the level of education achieved. It is determined by the acts of kindness demonstrated in daily life, whether by empathy or sheer will in the absence of empathy.

6. The primary meaning of life is wrapped around the kindness we show to others, even in the absence of reciprocity.

> You can help someone without loving them, but you can't love someone without helping them.

7. **Life's mixed metaphors**: It's great to have the eye of the tiger and the heart of a lion. But without a heart of gold, an empty shell remains.

8. To love beyond the self—beyond the family, beyond friendship, and beyond sympathy—is to know the true meaning of love because one must summon the will to act lovingly in the absence of feeling. It is a difficult art form seldom practiced.

9. Imagine, if you will, what a wonderful world this would be if everyone thought that everybody's child was *everybody's* child.

10. Those who are unlovable are still loveworthy. And those who can love the unlovable are the most loveworthy.

11. "Let Your Love Flow" is a 1976 single by the Bellamy Brothers. It was an international hit and reached #1 in several countries, including the United States. For sure, it's a love song; we all get the romantic angle. But don't let that view limit your overall interpretation. For me, the song is a metaphor of *love's universal power*, and especially the love for all living things. My favorite lines are in the chorus, and they can be understood as all-inclusive. (*Search on YouTube with lyrics.*)

12. Be kind and feel good . . . be kinder and feel better.

13. Love is a widespread concept that permeates the world's religions—it incorporates kindness, mercy, justice, charity, and forgiveness. In Hinduism, Buddhism, and Jainism, to name a few, some of those sentiments prevail. Additionally, respect and do no harm—known as ahimsa—is extended to all living creatures (a sentiment I cherish).

14. Tenderhearted tears are the unmasking of the soul; they are the crystal pearls from those who care.

15. You can help someone without loving them, but you can't love someone without helping them.

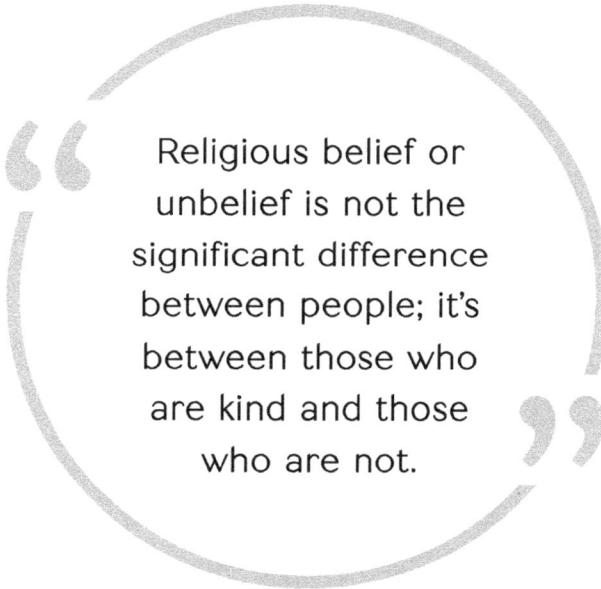

> " Religious belief or unbelief is not the significant difference between people; it's between those who are kind and those who are not. "

16. Prosperous people can afford to be happy during the holiday season. Poverty tends to nullify that luxury. But kindhearted people are inclined to be happy, regardless of the season, regardless of their means.

17. The one necessary ingredient that turns lust to true love is time.

18.There is nothing more productive than the extraordinary mind of an extraordinary person. And yet, there is nothing *more important* than the extraordinary kindness of an ordinary person.

> The road to heaven is paved with acts of kindness, not belief.

19. It is ironic that religions spearhead the concepts of love and forgiveness but often fail to promote inclusiveness. It's like a peanut butter and jelly sandwich without the jelly. I am thankful for progressive Christianity that counters that failing, albeit an outlier.

20. **Tough love:** For optimum results, loving a child wholistically requires the application of rational discipline.

21. **The Good Samaritan conundrum:** Part of my well-being is based on the good feelings derived when helping those whose well-being is not so well. What would I do without them?

22. You can't love anyone the same way you love anyone else—it's impossible.

23. The road to heaven is paved with acts of kindness, not belief.

(Flashback Vol. 1)

Be kind—everyone you know and everyone you meet is fighting a battle!

MARRIAGE

The Woman

There was a young woman who wanted a mate.
She met her true lover by chance or by fate.
The vows were exchanged without caution or fears.
They were married together for many good years.

But time is a taker they soon became old.
He died but he left her with memories untold.
She grew to be famous 'cause everyone knew,
She became the old woman who lived in a shoe.

Her children of course are not part of this poem.
'Cause the lady is old and the children are grown.

1. **A golden metaphor:** Thinking that you have found your soul mate can be a disappointing illusion. It is akin to the California gold rush when some of the 49ers thought they had found gold, only to discover it was fool's gold after all. Honestly, I think most of us are more like pyrite than gold. But

we're not losers. During the 1980s, researchers discovered that pyrite contains gold . . . it's just harder to extract, that's all.

2. More often than not, lovers are sharing reciprocal mirages. But occasionally they bond together in a life-sharing oasis.

3. You don't have to settle when you're looking for your soul mate, but you do have to come to terms.

4. **A Broken Wing:** Historically, the subjugation of women is appalling. Physical violence, mental abuse, and condescending attitudes against women have been the norm worldwide. Even in some of the most advanced first-world countries, women have not reached gender equality. But as we have discovered around the globe, given half a chance, a woman is any man's equal. Women are now excelling in all disciplines once privy only to men. Tangentially, the following 1998 Number One single about spousal abuse—"A Broken Wing"—comes from country singer Martina McBride. But for me, this song reflects much more than spousal abuse. I see it as a powerful metaphor that symbolizes the resilience and tenacity of women. History is replete with such examples. I honestly tear up at the chorus when I think of all the women who, despite the odds against them, have managed to overcome the disadvantages that men have imposed. But I'm also aware of women worldwide who still suffer under extreme subjugation. On a different note, I recall my mom having to work a 40-hour week while raising three little ones; my father was killed when I was four. Everyone has their own story. I

think this song—especially the chorus—will resonate with almost everyone in different ways, historically and personally. *(Search for "A Broken Wing" on YouTube with lyrics.)*

5. It was the champion boxer Muhammed Ali who coined the phrase "different strokes for different folks." That phrase should be part of the wedding ceremony when exchanging vows.

> More often than not, lovers are sharing reciprocal mirages. But occasionally they bond together in a life-sharing oasis.

6. **Divorce**: Once you give away the store, you can't go back to claim the goods.

7. A husband who gives his wife a waffle iron on their first wedding anniversary will suffer rookie consequences. He may get some tasty waffles, but his love life is bound to be flatter than a pancake.

8. **Spousal abuse**: Hell hath no fury like a woman scorned . . . except for a man who in like fashion has been disparaged.

9. **Numbers:** They say that "two can live cheaper than one." That's true if you're talking finance. But the real question is: Can two living together be happier than one? That depends on the two.

10. **The package:** The bees are beckoned to the payoff by the fragrance of colorful flowered packages. Humans are beckoned to the payoff by the beautiful wrappings of youthful looks and raging hormones. There's excitement and joy in that alluring experience. However, what's inside the package ultimately determines the viability of the goods. Unlike the satisfied bees, almost half of those human gift-wraps are surprise packages.

(Flashback Vol. 1)
Before the invention of glasses, midlife divorces were minimal.

MYSTERY/ENIGMA

The Enigmatic

We are a small-scale species
on a small-scale planet
in a midsize galaxy.

We don't know where we came from,
and we know not where we'll go.
It is more than common knowledge
that it's not for us to know.

Yet we look for signs that whisper
to our dull restricted minds,
while the Mystery still entices
with tenacity that binds.

1. **Believer, agnostic, atheist:** The Mystery is undefinable no matter what we believe or don't believe. In this regard, we are all splashing around in an ocean of speculation, and

I don't believe anyone is without a lifejacket (whatever the truth may be).

2. In the biblical Book of Ecclesiastes (3:19, 21), we hear the old prophet saying: "For the fate of humans and the fate of animals is the same; as one dies, so dies the other.... Who knows whether the spirit goes upward and the spirit of animals goes downward to the earth?" Indeed, who knows! Accordingly, I like the song "Let the Mystery Be" by Iris DeMint. *(Search on YouTube with lyrics.)*

3. Do Mother Nature's antithetical creations—beauty and the ugly—indicate the absence of a God as traditionally conceived? Don't tell me it's not a mystery.

4. **Perspective:** We live on a grisly death planet—kill or be killed is the key to survival. Even if we agree that death is essential, *why must death be levied in such painful and disgusting ways?* If I were God, I think I could have come up with a better blueprint for the natural order. What does that tell you about me? It should tell you that if I believed what I just suggested, I should be classified as an arrogant, ignorant, if not stupid, human being. Nevertheless, pervasive pain and suffering does make one wonder about the Mystery.

5. **The enigma:** There are only two cogent explanations for our existence: (1) It is a mystery that has meaning beyond our understanding, or (2) It is a mystery without meaning. The former is a possibility, the latter is forever perplexing and insufferable.

6. This one puzzles me: Aside from joyous reunions, what would be the purpose of eternal life? Whether or not one agrees, Mormons are the front runners on this one.

7. **Vale of tears**: Pain and suffering on all levels of the animal kingdom are part of the natural order. Aside from our self-inflicted hardships, why do we suffer and are sometimes forced to endure bouts of extreme affliction? This conundrum has been debated by the most learned religious and philosophical minds from time immemorial, and supposedly explained by religious bodies worldwide. Yet, there are no answers that satisfy. I can add nothing to help clarify this enigma.

> Aside from religious speculation, no one knows where the universe came from. We may know something about its beginnings, but no one knows why it got started or why we're here.

8. **A Christian enigma**: No matter how you rationalize the numbers, a Trinity—Father, Son, and Holy Spirit—does not constitute monotheism, any more than a plural constitutes a singular. However, we can contemplate that a truth can exist beyond human logic.

9. **A perplexing mystery**: Aside from religious speculation, no one knows where the universe came from. We may know something about its beginnings, but no one knows why it got started or why we're here. However, through the sciences of astronomy and astrobiology, we now know that the universe has a definite life span. Still, no one knows what happens after its demise . . . if anything.

10. Is it God that works in mysterious ways or is it our lack of knowledge that creates that cause-and-effect assumption? I concede that it could be both.

11. The most essential prerequisite for exploring the spiritual realm is the elimination of certitude.

(Flashback Vol. 1)
Can we acknowledge and respect the God/Mystery without worshipping it?

MYTHOLOGY

Religious Myth

The story and message of myths,
Are as old as the old monoliths.
They're highly unusual
and come with surprises,
And somehow reveal
what no one surmises.

A myth, some will argue,
is never historic.
But the essence of myth
lives on in the story.
Whatever the genre,
whatever the plot,
the myth is the best way
enigma is taught.

1. For most people, even after the Enlightenment of the seventeenth century, the New Testament genres of story, history and myth remained intertwined as one. Consequently, New

Testament mythology continues to be conflated with history in a literal sense, as opposed to its parabolic teaching. The inability to untangle these conflated components has created a serious stumbling block for a proper understanding of the text, while alienating a more enlightened public.

2. **Hindsight**: Ancient theology is today's mythology—will today's theology be tomorrow's mythology?

> New Testament mythology continues to be conflated with history in a literal sense, as opposed to its parabolic teaching.

3. *The conformity of belief within the confines of insufficient knowledge leads to the illusion that one possesses truthful concepts.* This helps to explain the suicidal folly at Jonestown and Heaven's Gate, what led the German people to follow Hitler, and the witch hunts in medieval Europe, to name a few. This also helps to explain why people of the first-century AD believed fervently in mythology. They believed that one could be possessed by demons, that women could be impregnated by the gods, that virgin births were plausible, and that savior gods could descend and ascend between Heaven and Earth. Please read my first sentence again.

4. If Christianity is to survive in the long run, it must overcome three obstacles. First, it must extricate itself from right-wing evangelicalism which, in many respects, flies in the face of the New Testament (NT). Second, Christians must get in line with both historical and religious mainline scholars as they continue to convincingly demythologize the NT. (Mythology is one of the helping signposts of religion, but becomes problematic if taken literally.) Third, Christians must come to appreciate scripture as inspired, but not infallible.

5. **Unenlightened screenwriters**: Unfortunately, religious Hollywood movies literalize first-century mythology.

6. Children's fairytales are about imaginary beings and lands (Santa Claus, Wizard of Oz, Superman, etc.). We don't take them literally, but they often convey truthful or inspiring lessons beyond their entertainment. The adult version of the fairytale is called mythology. Myths enshrine supernatural ideas (virgin births, resurrections, creation narratives, etc.). They, too, convey possible truths and lessons beyond historical necessity. But unlike fairytales, myths are intertwined with historical people and places. This makes it terribly hard for persons to make a distinction between myth and history within the storyline. As a result, laypeople interpret the entire story literally. That's a problem. It creates a tensional line of thought incompatible with twenty-first century awareness. Consequently, it undermines the authenticity of the story's historical elements and obscures the parabolic nature of the myth.

7. The mythical parable about eating the forbidden fruit from the Tree of Knowledge of Good and Evil in the Garden of Eden didn't instigate the downfall of man; on the contrary, it was humanity's gateway into reality.

8. Religious myths are figurative stories and concepts that form the bridge between our present life and the afterlife. They place meat on the bones of our supernatural imaginings. They are constructive models that metaphorically help us to presuppose our origins, give us hope, and help us navigate the mystery of the unknown.

(Flashback Vol. 1)
For the sake of Christianity's survival, the Church hierarchy must begin to explore with their people the value and richness of biblical myth-messaging rather than constructing make-believe shrines to literal interpretations of wishful improbabilities.

NATURE

The Tree

Today I planted a Ficus tree
For future birds I'll never see.
A little shade when it grows tall,
For many a critter big and small.

Today I planted a Ficus tree,
A gift for the many I'll never see.
This flora my heart of hearts has ordered,
Has brought me joy to pay it forward.

1. **Nature's antithetical:** Folks find it easy to spotlight the splendor in nature's theater, while turning down the house-lights on its opposite. Personally, I am thrilled and spiritually uplifted by the wonders of nature, yet equally baffled by its ever-present violence and brutality.

2. With God, all things are possible but not probable. The ordained laws of nature take precedence. Predictability

is fixed. If it were not so, the world would not be consistently ordered. Confirmation of this truth is in the eye of the fair-minded.

3. **A metaphoric consideration:** From the day we are born until the day we die we are dodging nature's bullets. In our youth, she fires a single-shot .22 caliber rifle. At midlife, the caliber and ammunition capacity changes, and we are faced with a semi-automatic rifle. In our old age, nature opens up with a machine gun, and we know there's a kill shot on the way. Nevertheless, I'm thankful—thankful that I didn't fall prey to the .22 caliber.

4. Nature's laws appear to be impersonal and consistent. To what degree they are manipulated by the gods, if at all, remains an issue vigorously debated by some. That said, the observable evidence seems to support seventeenth-century Deism. Believers would beg to differ by offering awe-inspiring interpretations of the natural order. Whatever the case, when it comes to supernatural intervention, the argument remains *unprovable* either way.

5. Waking up every morning unencumbered is a blessing, no matter the age. But making it through the day unscathed is even more so.

6. Humans are the existential threat to all of life on Earth, but the laws of Mother Nature are the existential threat that will eventually wipe out not only the Earth—but also the

entire universe! Good news: I suspect there's a follow-up act in the wings.

7. Birds and butterflies are Mother Nature's materialized rainbows.

> Personally, I am thrilled and spiritually uplifted by the wonders of nature, yet equally baffled by its ever-present violence and brutality.

8. **Our nature:** Sometimes we say that humans are inhuman, as if to imply that's not really who we are. However, being inhuman is a part of our human makeup. It appears that nature burdens us with the inclination to be cruel and barbaric, while nurture mitigates those tendencies. In short, we are the end result of what nature and nurture have made us. Regrettably, nature will take precedence if nurture fails to dominate.

(Flashback Vol. 1)

The beauty and wonderment of this glorious "natural order" is blurred by our 24/7 round-the-clock exposure to it. Therefore, it is incumbent upon us to revive our sleepy spirits. We must reopen our eyes to nature's magnificence lest those neglected spaces in our hearts remain vacant.

OFFBEAT

The Clock

You say my face would stop a clock
that wasn't said politely.
And then you say it's just a joke
don't take it so precisely.

I understand it's just a joke
and everything's in fun.
But just in case you're serious
your face would make one run.

1. Life is like the game of pool. Sometimes you're the eight ball. Sometimes you're the cue ball. Sometimes you're just one of the other balls. But what you really want to be is the cue stick.

2. Stay in your own lane—it's easy to get run over if you cross into someone else's.

3. Attrition: Sometimes people will say they're killing time, but it's time that's killing them.

4. I'm wondering if desert *nomads* ever get angry.

5. Pick any occupation or genre: You must be consistently average to be good. You must be consistently good to be great. You must be consistently great to be one of the best. You must be consistently one of the best to be the best.

6. They say, "Imitation is the sincerest form of flattery." In some cases, however, it's a form of hijacking for lack of originality.

> 66
>
> Sometimes people will say they're killing time, but it's time that's killing them.
>
> 99

7. *The New York Times* reports that Melissa Gilbert (from *Little House on the Prairie* fame) was arrested and convicted on charges of fraud. The title of the article read: "Melissa Gilbert goes from the Little House to the Big House." Attention : I concocted that joke; not a true story.

8. They say that great minds think alike. Unfortunately, so do poor ones.

9. The best four words to use in the middle of a discussion with someone you don't agree with are, "You may be right." Thereafter, your opinion is more likely to be fairly considered. Such a ploy is not manipulative if you're open to the possibility that they may be right.

10. My greatness is surpassed only by my humility.

11. **A play on words**: Has a man called Nicolas lost more money than a man who is penniless?

12. **Oldies but goodies**: The Four Tops are an American vocal quartet and are one of the best early groups that helped create the Motown sound. From 1953—1997, they had a total of 24 hits on the *Billboard Hot 100*. In 1988, while in London, they were scheduled on Pan Am flight 103 back to New York. They were delayed and missed their flight. That delay was a stroke of incredibly good luck. Flight 103 carried a bomb that exploded over the Scottish town of Lockerbie, killing all 259 passengers, and 11 people on the ground. That's one lesson I keep in mind when I get impatient for missing a green light. You just never know.

13. Sometimes I'm predictable, sometimes I'm not. Does that mean I'm predictably unpredictable, or unpredictably predictable?

14. **Regrets:** If you can't fix it, don't fixate on it.

15. Stay in your own league—it's hard to hit a homerun in someone else's ballpark.

16. **2024:** If we can win more Olympic medals than any other country in the world, why don't we have a gold medal for cyber security against foreign and domestic hackers? That might be a poor analogy, but the question holds.

17. It's very taxing to drive down memory lane if you've had a lot of accidents along the way.

18. I don't believe that American democracy is the beginning and the end of all things political, but I lean in that direction. I don't believe that Christianity is the beginning and the end of all things religious, but I lean in that direction. In other words, *I believe in the right of preference*, while recognizing and respecting the rights of others who differ in their preferences—assuming, of course, that those choices do not harm or interfere with civil and human rights.

19. **Below the waterline:** Even when we see the problem coming, it may be too late. After all, it wasn't the tip of the iceberg that sank the Titanic.

(Flashback Vol. 1)
Life has been hard on me. I had to learn from other people's mistakes because I never made any of my own.

PERSONAL DIARY
(True Reflections)

The Captive

I'm a prisoner between the before and hereafter.
I journey through life knowing not what comes after.
I am tied to the present the span between tides.
The past is the past and tomorrow still hides.

1. I feel terrible about the mistakes I made as a teenager. But then again, my brain wasn't fully developed. I feel even worse about the mistakes I made after it was.

2. Compared to some, I have achieved much. Compared to others, I have achieved little. In either case, the time continuum will erase it all or stick it in the vault of obsolescence. Maybe my Ernie-isms will survive. You may laugh, but it's comforting to be self-delusional.

3. Today, I got a call from an old friend I hadn't heard from in years. That made my day. I also got a call from an old friend that I hear from almost every day. That also made my day.

4. I know I can't fix all the world's problems; but sitting on the sidelines might make me one of them.

5. Why does survival depend on one life form killing another life form? It's a terrible violent blueprint. I'm always killing something—if only by proxy—just to stay alive. If there is an Infinite Wisdom beyond our temporal understanding—and I choose to believe there is—I'll have plenty of questions to ask.

6. **My eclectic rainbow:** I am not a dogmatic Christian, but I do embrace most of Christianity's non-mythical teachings. In addition, Unitarianism, Deism, Hinduism, Buddhism, Jainism, pantheism, panentheism, humanism, and agnosticism play into my mental assortment of tensional philosophical goodies.

7. We are strapped-in passengers on the Ferris wheel of life, subject to the rise and fall of unpredictable fortune. I'm grateful for the ride. My life has generally been on the upswing. I will admit, however, that the Ferris wheel metaphor is lacking. The ups and downs of life are not uniformly distributed.

8. **English:** Sometimes I overrule the grammar police. Why? Because I think it's more important to be reader-friendly than grammatically principled. (In case you didn't notice, I just gave myself a perfect excuse for any incorrect punctuation you might notice.)

9. We don't always practice what we preach. Nevertheless, good advice in the absence of virtuous behavior is still valuable.

10. In 1999, at the age of 60, just before I started teaching at Glendale Community College, I visited the Arizona State University library. Like many elders of my generation, I was not well versed with the digital age. I never had a computer, but I didn't see that as a problem. After searching out the ASU library, I ended up at the information desk monitored by a young student. "Excuse me," I said, "but I can't find the card catalogue section." She looked at me inquisitively and asked: "The what section?" Thereafter, I went to the Apple Store and bought an iMac.

11. **Count your blessings**: Without a good dose of serendipity, my life could have been humdrum at best, and a disaster at worst.

12. **Compound running**: I started jogging when I was 28, about 57 years ago. I have averaged at least 60 miles a month (720 miles per year). Over my lifetime that adds up to 41,000 miles. The distance between Los Angeles and New York City is 2,797 road miles. Round trip is double that (5,594 miles). That means I have logged enough miles to have run back and forth across this country 7 times!

13. It serves no purpose to fret over the loss of our glory days, where the sweetness of youth once reigned. I like the ending sentiment from the actress Natalie Wood in the 1961 movie, *Splendor in the Grass:* "Though nothing can bring back the splendor in the grass, glory in the flower, we will grieve not—rather find strength in what remains behind."

14. Doris Day was a consummate American actress and singer. From 1947 to 1967 she recorded more than 650 songs, several of which were number-one hits. Her signature song was "Que Sera, Sera." Her films were even more successful and included the many genres of musicals, comedies, and dramas. I first met Doris Day in 1963 at the Daywin offices in Beverly Hills. She was a charming lady, and I had a nice conversation with her. I would soon be headed for graduate studies at United Seminary in Ohio, and she wished me well. Doris Day died in 2019 at the age of 97. I'm 84 years old and, according to the actuaries, I'm already past my sell-by date. This all has reminded me of a cute little ditty I heard her sing back in 1950 when I was ten. I present it here for your consideration and reflection. *(Search for "Enjoy Yourself" on YouTube with lyrics.)*

15. My greatness was stymied by my inability to be great! Fortunately, my mediocrity was stymied by my inability to be mediocre.

16. **Optimist:** When I was growing up in the 1940s and 50s, there was only one major taxi company (Yellow Cab), only one telephone company (AT&T/Ma Bell), only one reliable ballpoint pen (Paper Mate), only one cola diet drink (Diet Rite Cola), only three TV stations (ABC, CBS & NBC), only one music chart (The Hit Parade), only two best-selling cars (Ford & Chevy) . . . AND NO MASS SHOOTINGS. I like to reminisce, but I enjoy the present and look forward to the future (most of the time).

17. When I was young, I thought that when I came face to face with the Grim Reaper, I would spit in his eye. *Take that!* Now that I'm old, I've decided that the best way to approach him is facing backwards.

> " We are strapped-in passengers on the Ferris wheel of life, subject to the rise and fall of unpredictable fortune. I'm grateful for the ride. "

18. My beliefs about the supernatural remain unclear. This ambivalence is based on my lifelong accumulated experiences with world religions, nature, education, and personal relationships. But my beliefs—or disbeliefs—cannot, do not, and will not, serve the needs of the many. At best, they may only serve as steppingstones for the dos and don'ts of future seekers.

19. I was moved by the song "For a Dancer." It was written by Rock and Roll Hall of Fame inductee Jackson Browne. He wrote this song for one of his close friends who died in a fire but the lyrics have universal appeal. It's a profound introspection of the reoccurring struggle we have in trying to understand death. It's a sad song, for sure. But it also expresses a thanks for the benefits we have derived from others that turned us into dancers, with added encouragement to do the same for others. It is one of my favorite songs. Enough said. Make of it what you will. (*Search on YouTube with lyrics.*)

20. I just picked up a prescription from my pharmacist. This one's for a muscle spasm. Honestly, half of the time I don't even use these prescriptions. I just read about the possible side effects, and my symptoms disappear.

21. I don't know about you, but here is an exercise I've been practicing all my life. And I've got this one down to a science: would've, could've, should've.

22. In 1955, when I was fifteen, a Disney movie called *Lady and the Tramp* showed up at our local theatre. It was an animated romantic adventure tale about a sheltered uptown cocker spaniel and a streetwise downtown mutt. What a hoot. I loved it. I purchased the soundtrack and saw the movie 26 times over a period of weeks. This is one I'll not share with my psychiatrist.

23. **2023:** My computer has been acting up and my printer no longer works. I'm blaming it on the Chinese spy balloon.

24. Just before my first aortic valve replacement, I asked my surgeon about the survival rate for this type of surgery. He said the national average showed that only one out of 3000 didn't survive. Obviously, I inquired about his survival ratio. He told me that he had never lost a patient after doing 2,999 surgeries.

25. I'm a lot more into analog than I am digital because I'm a lot older than I am younger.

26. **Classroom antics:** After retiring from the United Methodist Church, I spent 21 years teaching religious studies at Glendale Community College. Under their auspices five of those years were spent at ASU. I worked hard at making the classroom experience fun for my students. I was humorous and a jokester at heart. Anyway, I'm proud to say that my student evaluations were extraordinary, and I was one of only two instructors in our department with a 5-star rating. Here is one of those evaluations that I think is quintessential: "Ernie is an amazing instructor. He knows his stuff. We all love him. But the dude is crazy."

27. We have too many overweight children. They just don't get enough exercise. When we were kids in the 1950s, we were constantly up and down from a sitting position to a standing position a hundred times a day. And each time we had to walk all the way across the room to flip the TV channel.

28. We are better informed through the ages, yet perpetually ignorant. I try to keep that in mind when I consider my worldview to be well grounded.

> "
>
> My greatness was stymied by my inability to be great! Fortunately, my mediocrity was stymied by my inability to be mediocre.
>
> "

29. As I was driving along on a side street, I spotted two adult quails crossing in front of me. Between the momma and poppa were a string of seven tiny dots. Of course, I stopped to avoid hitting the family. They all got across safely except for the littlest one who, try as he may, couldn't jump above the curb. I quickly got out of the car, went over, and gently scooped the little guy up. After setting him down on the ground, he scurried off to his onlooking family that had taken shelter under a bush. It seemed to be a celebrative moment for all. Indeed, that experience was a thrill, a joy, and a blessing.

30. My grandparents were born running against the wind. They escaped the Mexican Civil War in 1916 when they crossed the USA border with my six-month-old mother in

tow. God bless America, and all other countries willing to accept refugees.

31. When it comes to religion or atheism, I don't live in either world of black or white dogma. I live in-between. I live in a gray dimension that offers more ambiguity than certainty. Please do not confuse my metaphor with the "sitting on the fence" metaphor. There is no fence . . . at least not in this expansive gray area. And I find myself moving between the black and white borders with a flexible mindset not experienced in the other two realms.

32. I got my courage up and went to the gym today. I'm proud to say that I was on the stationary bike for about an hour. That has encouraged me to come back tomorrow, and this time I'm going to pedal.

33. **The attitude of certitude:** I remain indebted to my university and seminary education that liberated me from unbridled religious dogmatism. Of course, one might argue that I have simply adopted a different form of dogmatism. But one thing I know for sure: I feel a whole lot better having discarded the attitude of certitude that had placed my religious beliefs in a straitjacket.

34. This morning I sprinkled some seed for my mourning doves, and that made my day. I saw some beautiful cloud formations, and that made my day. I had a wonderful cheese enchilada lunch, and that made my day. I had a receptive group of students, and that made my day. I had a good

workout at the gym, and that made my day. I conversed with a dear friend, and that made my day. I gave some cash to a homeless person, and that made my day. I saw two young lovers kissing in the park, and that made my day. I came home and turned on the news, and that almost ruined my day.

35. **Yikes**: When I was in seminary working on my master's degree, the faculty had the students put on a talent show. The school's worn-out sound system wasn't that great, but I gave it a shot. I sang an old 1950s hillbilly song called "Sally Let Your Bangs Hang Down." Following the program, one of my professors approached me to ask why I had chosen that song, which he thought was inappropriate. That puzzled me. It wasn't until a few days later that I found out what the students and profs had heard on that dime-store sound system: "Sally Let Your Pants Hang Down."

36. During my teenage years, the song "Love is a Many-Splendored Thing" reached number one on Billboard in 1955. It won the Academy Award for Best Original Song in 1956. Looking back on my juvenile love life, I would have to retitle the song: "Love is a Many-Splintered Thing."

37. **"Glory Days"**: I was thumbing through my 1957 high school yearbook and started wondering where all those young faces ended up. Aside from two good friends, I wasn't sure how many of my peers were still alive in this year of 2024, nor what they had accomplished in life. In contemplation, the ghost of high school past came roaring back. I played junior varsity football, I was on the Honor Society roll, and

I was a popular jokester with my peers. But I never achieved that topnotch popularity that some of our jocks and homecoming queens received. For sure, those HS days are memorable, but most of us had not yet reached our glory days. However, for those who did, we can only hope that HS wasn't the end of their exaltation. If that was the zenith of someone's life, that would be a sad commentary indeed. (From 1985, here's "Glory Days" by Bruce Springsteen. The ending may be too long, but the chorus and lyrics are vintage.) *(Search on YouTube with lyrics.)*

38. **Unorthodox**: Although the idea of "God" still tumbles around in my head like a cement mixer, I do not define God in any traditional manner. In fact, I am not at all comfortable with the term, God. At worst, it's an antiquated expression that conveys primitive notions. At best, it's a theoretical reach for the ultimate Mystery that vibrantly resonates within our imaginings. I prefer the latter.

39. **November 2024**: Our summer here in Phoenix, Arizona, was blistering hot! We shattered over a dozen all-time heat records. We had a record number of 110-degree days, and many were higher. We also broke the record of over-100-degree days in a row. Overall, we had the hottest summer on record. Finally, this week, our temp dropped to 80. It's very difficult getting used to this cold weather.

40. I believe in God (a supernatural reality), but I don't claim to know there is one. If you don't believe in God, you shouldn't claim to know there isn't one.

41. **Copycat mind readers:** I would not be comfortable having a twin brother. We would certainly look alike, and that wouldn't be good for either of us. But I wonder how closely we would think alike. Wouldn't there always be a gnawing suspicion of: "Is he thinking what I'm thinking?" Uh-oh . . .

42. I'll soon be 86. I'm at the age where I really don't mind if people finish my sentences.

43. I guess I need to confess. I have an addiction and I just don't have the will to break it. I guess we're all addicted to something, but this one haunts me. God help me; I'm addicted to life.

(Flashback Vol. 1)
I don't believe that the universe is 'godless.' But I do believe it is godless in the way we imagine 'god' to be.

NOTE: Many of my own personal feelings, shortcomings, and world-views are apparent in the other segments of this work.

PHILOSOPHY

The Thinker

Some folks don't like philosophy.
Some say it's worse than broccoli.
Some say it's an atrocity,
or like a colonoscopy

I find it to be none of those
and I would argue and suppose
cerebral stretch with less repose
is how our knowledge grows and grows,
as any thinking person knows.

1. The Chinese philosophy of yin and yang in the religion of Taoism serves as a black and white symbol of good and evil (a form of dualism in human nature). But it's a misread if we see this configuration as mainly good with a little bad, or mainly bad with a little good. Perhaps Hitler and Mother Teresa fit those extremes. However, for most of us, the black

and white dots are neither equivalent in size, nor equally distributed. (Note: Yin and yang have various applications and interpretations.)

2. "All good things must come to an end." However, I take comfort in knowing that the flip side of that idiom is also true.

> We should
> not think of ourselves
> as masters of any animal,
> wild or domesticated.
> We may be their
> guardians, but never
> their masters.

3. I'm not the man I was when I wore a younger man's clothes. I'm not the man I'll be when I wear an older man's clothes. In Buddhism, this is known as the philosophy of impermanence and impersonality; *people are in a constant state of change (which happens to be true—physically, and mentally).* Give this some serious thought because the implications are profound. Since I'm

not who I was and I'm not who I'll be, and I'm in a constant state of change, then who am I? Or when am I? Or what am I? Or am I?

4. Artificial intelligence is man-made. If we did not exist, AI would not exist. Although we are mixing apples with oranges, this still begs the question: If AI cannot originate without human intelligence, how can human intelligence originate without a superior counterpart? Stated differently: Can intelligence evolve from non-intelligence, be it artificial or biological?

> "
> Artificial intelligence is man-made. If we did not exist, AI would not exist. Can intelligence evolve from non-intelligence, be it artificial or biological?
> "

(Flashback Vol. 1)

The philosophy of inequality: We should not think of ourselves as masters of any animal, wild or domesticated. We may be their guardians, but never their masters. The idea that intellectual superiority lends greater inherent worth to humans is a primitive misguided concept. Likewise, the idea of a soul that is unique to humans is equally misleading. This biased religious and intellectual hierarchy of classification diminishes the intrinsic value of all other living creatures, separates us from the natural order, and overlooks the pervasiveness of relativism beyond Earth's boundaries. It is more than probable that somewhere within the existing three trillion galaxies there are life forms that are far superior to us. Should we ever become subject to their influence, we can only pray that their thinking has evolved beyond the philosophy of inequality that we unthinkingly believe and practice. If not, it is within this universal marketplace that we will be weighed in the balance and found wanting.

POEMS (ADDITIONAL)

What's Poetry

My friend and I we disagree
As he prefers a verse that's free.
He doesn't like the rhyming line
Or syncopated rhythmic time.

I tried to tell him once or twice
That free verse isn't all that nice.
But he prefers unmatching prose,
And to all else he turns his nose,
And why he does nobody knows.

Not even alternating lines
Will he appreciate the rhymes.
He doesn't care for symmetry.
He says it isn't poetry.

I try to help him see the light
But he thinks rhyming verse is trite.
He screams and hollers and he rants.
I get so scared I wet my pants.

The Poet

I'm not a poet with words that are lofty,
And poets of merit will call me a softy.
But nevertheless, my words will be ample
The verse below will be my example.

> Every cloud has a silver lining
> That's only true when the sun is shining.
> But during the dark night of the soul
> When all is black as black as coal
> We search in vain for the silver lining
> Until again the sun is shining.

Now you may think those words are shallow
And I will agree they don't ring hallow.
Even so, my words are ample
The verse above was my example.

A Love Poem

For you I will pen this original poem,
Before I must leave for the old people's home.
I guess there is nothing that I can do,
Except to say goodbye to you.
I'm very glad the time was ample,
For me to leave this artsy sample.

Ammit

Her paws would glide across the ground
Her stride was swift and steady.

Her fur was gold, her eyes were brown,
Her face was slightly ruddy.

She came to me unknowingly.
I came to love her so.
But death came rushing suddenly,
I had to let her go.

I held her close and kissed her
when we said our last goodbye.
She seemed resigned and stoic,
With a glimmer in her eye.

The world is now a darker place,
Her absence so severe.
There's just no hint, or any trace,
Of one I loved so dear.

The day will soon be coming
When I'll leave this world behind.
I'll hug her on that someday
If the gods are so inclined.

Colorful Antics

They say that nothing rhymes with orange,
Well I am here to prove them wrong.
And long before this poem is over
They will sing a different song.

I won't keep you in suspense,
I won't even make you tense.

It's not hard to rhyme with orange,
When we have a fruit called orange.
Case closed.
(*I think this one reflects my Ernie-ism fatigue.*)

Today

When the cat's away the mouse will play,
What are we going to do today?
What do you think, and what do you say,
What are we going to do today?

A little of this, a little of that,
Put on your coat and grab your hat.
We're off to the races for good-time places,
To have some fun with good-time faces.

This next poem was written when I was a teenager (1959),
with slight editing in 2024.
My 1948 Grammar School Field Trip to San Pedro
LA Waterfront at the Port of Los Angeles.

The Dog With No Name

When first my eyes upon her fell
Asleep and friendless I could tell.
Her shaggy hair was dirty brown,
Her paws adjacent to the ground.

My footsteps close, she then awoke,
Her eyes how sad and lonely spoke.

With gentle effort she arose
And took my measure with her nose.

I saw the hunger in her face,
She shared my lunch as in a race.
We kept the day with bonded heart,
But knew not yet we had to part.

My years they numbered only nine.
Decision making was not mine.
They would not let me take her home.
I knew once more she'd be alone.

What could I say, what could I do,
My time to leave was all I knew.
She could not guess the where or why,
Nor could I tell her though I try.

To board the bus, I broke the trust,
To leave her at the door I must.
I moved along and took my place,
And through the window saw her face.

I tried to smile and say goodbye,
In vain I struggled not to cry.
There are no words that can express,
Her anxious look and my distress.

The bus now rolling without pause,
And right behind ran little paws.

She ran as fast as she could run,
But to me there she could not come.

And soon we left her far behind
A haunting memory so unkind.
That night beside my bed I knelt.
A sad and lonely boy I felt.

So now these words come to an end,
The pain remains, I won't pretend.
I struggle still, but deem it best,
To think my friend is now at rest.

The Unfortunate

I can't complain I won't despair,
not even with the loss of hair.
Such trivial woes do not compare,
with those whose life is so unfair.

Emergence

In the human deck of cards,
where Jacks and Queens
and lofty kings
are found in juxtaposition,
I saw you as the Queen of hearts,
without the pomp and circumstance,
awaiting disposition.

    But not for me.

I loved you from afar.
Proximity denied.
And yet the pundits say
that the owner of a lonely heart
can still find respite from afar.
    But not for me.

When children fly on
playgrounds swings,
their laughter and
their vibrant screams
may echo once again
in the turbulence of erotic love
that awaits their future years.
    But not for me.

Still, I envy them not.
I do not aim to be unkind,
but their union of forever
is an illusion of the mind.
Aspirations of the heart
cannot soar on the wings
of wanton desire.
Their coming together lurches
into the primal passion of the flesh.
Carnal lust gone amuck,
and by itself is not enough.
    Not for me.

Deception rules when they pretend
that they won't falter in the end.

But in the final climax
of their togetherness,
they will come to understand
the emptiness of nothingness.
    But not for me.

Their hopeful dreams
are FORNEVER.
What's that you say,
there's no such word as fornever?
Even so, I bring it forth as a contender.
    But not for me,
      for I have loved you eternally.

And yet, I cannot reach
across this earthly chasm.
It runs too deep,
and wide of breadth.
We are separated pilgrims,
traversing segregated ground.
We endure the absence of experience,
and the experience of absence.

Whatever bond we fashion here,
wilts like a flower
with a broken stem.
Yet in the afterlife to come,
we will emerge as one.
    But not for them.

Fill In The B_____s

The lazy are stuck in a rut.
What they need is a kick in the_____.
The rich are concerned about money.
Some cheat on their marital_____.

If the rules you refuse to obey
then to you I would earnestly_____,
at the risk of being too crass,
you are simply a pain in the_____.

The Pismire Ant

There once was a pismire ant,
who carried a negative slant.
He was always depressed,
like none of the rest,
and did nothing but grumble and rant.

There were giants above to reflect on.
And the odds of survival to bet on.
From the moment of birth,
made to crawl on the earth,
and he worried that he would be stepped on.

Now the pismire ant was afeared.
And for being a coward was jeered.
He was feared of the dark,
and the dog that would bark,
and he ran when the red ants appeared.

There was nothing but worry and strife.
He was willfully wasting his life.
But that suddenly changed,
when good fortune arranged,
bumping heads with his soon to be wife.

He would whistle and sing her a song.
She supported and made him feel strong.
As the evening grew dark,
and she wanted to spark,
she wore nothing at all but a thong.

He was smitten with love and he told her
as he hurried on over to hold her.
It was all night and day,
that she wanted to play,
they were hot and they never got colder.

Now the measure of life is not bending.
And we know that it's fragile and pending.
But they died growing old,
as I have been told,
so it's time for this poem to be ending.

But the pismire story is broken.
And we're left with a cynical token.
'Cause the narrative changed,
it was all rearranged,
and a pissant is all that is spoken.

Some Men

A man who breaks our mores,
be they legal, be they not,
is a maladjusted varmint
and will surely come to naught.

A man who is a racist
is deserving of disdain.
And is nothing but a weasel
going down the sewage drain.

A man who is a sexist
is a major rectal pain.
He is just a little jackass
with an even smaller brain.

Frosty the Snowman

I will say a few words about Frosty.
And I'll try not to make it too lofty.
He was white as a ghost,
to the children the most,
but like those made of snow was a softy.

He was jolly with never a frown.
He would frolic and dance through the town.
With the temperature low,
he could get up and go,
and would always be playing the clown.

Now Frosty was nothing but fun.
With the children in tow he would run.

But as everyone knows,
as the story now goes,
he could never endure in the sun.

Their love and respect he did earn.
But the children with sadness would learn.
When he said his goodbye,
all the children would cry,
but they stopped when he said he'd return.

Now this poem about Frosty ain't wrong.
But the story you see is too long.
I respectfully say,
that this isn't the way,
and that's why they have written a song.

The Enigma

The Mystery knows what we suppose.
Like prose it glows and throughout flows,
While speculation grows and grows.
And life with all its highs and lows,
Remains a mystery no one knows.

The Knight

*(My original teenage version from 1959 with some
problematic mixture of past and present tense)*

When I was young in the days of old,
When knights were in flower and courage was bold,
I'd ride on my stallion defending the right,
In armor as black and as cold as the night.

My horse and I'd rest at the water's edge,
And just for a moment recalling my pledge
As a knight for the king to whom I belong,
I'm defending his honor my oath and my song.

One day as I rode in a valley so green,
I spied a young knight who slighted my king.
At last it is challenged my honor and pride,
And so against evil my horse and I ride.

Black as his heart was his masculine steed.
We charged at each other with thundering speed.
I level my lance and aim at his chest
And know if I die it will be at my best.

At last we meet with a clashing sound,
What pain I feel as I fall to the ground.
His lance has pierced my armored plate,
I now await my deadly fate.

But no one comes as I struggle to rise,
Perhaps he awaits me with cruel laughing eyes.
At last I am up with my knife in my hand,
'Til the last breath I'll fight and die like a man.

Where is he this villain my vision is blurred?
I grow weaker and weaker oh death is assured.
Then just for a moment my focus is clear.
I sigh and I smile, 'twas a dead man I feared.
For there on the green with my lance in his chest
Was the knight who had tried and died at his best.

The light is now fading and as I go down,
How still and how quiet no whisper no sound.
For here in this valley, yes nature has seen
Two knights trade their lances and die on the green.
2024 Amendment:
It seems very strange and quite unknown,
how could a dead knight write this poem?

(Flashback Vol. 1)

On the Wing of a Bird

On the wing of a bird I imagined I flew,
As the sun barely rising made diamonds of dew.
There were rivers and mountains that I'd never seen,
And the valleys were covered with carpets of green.

My heart sang with laughter what joy if you knew
On the wing of a bird soaring into the blue.
We circled a mountain whose top to the sky
Brought mist and a roar from the waterfalls cry.

We perched on its crest in the heat of the day
Then glided on down to the cool of the spray.
We fluttered through sunshine then under a cloud,
And filtered through raindrops that fell in a crowd.
As radiant colors majestically flashed,

On the wing of a bird through the rainbow I crashed.
We followed the sun as it moved on its way
'Til the sunlight was fading the Earth turning gray.

But perhaps you are wondering or find it absurd,
That I could have flown on the wing of a bird.

POLITICS

Political Metaphor
(This poem from Vol 1)

Extremes are on the edges
    of a double-edged sword,
But the blade is in the middle
    and should never be ignored.
If you're too much to the left
    or you're too much to the right,
It's the truth within the middle
    that will make it just right.
Extremes are on the edges
    of a double-edged sword,
But the blade is in the middle
    and should never be ignored.

1. Going to a political rally is a bit like going to the movies. To enjoy the event, you must be willing to suspend reality.

2. **A double whammy:** It is clear that whatever cabinet and Supreme Court nominees declare under oath during their confirmation hearings, as opposed to what they do after confirmation, could serve as a dictionary's perfect definition

of hypocrisy. It is also clear that some senators confirm people based on excuses that serve their political interest, rather than what's best for the country. Obviously, we're getting a double dose of humbug.

3. Here are the four words you never hear between Republicans and Democrats when it comes to politics: "You may be right."

4. **Speeches:** Inspiring words without an inspiring voice is hardly inspiring.

5. Every time we have a presidential election, the opposition always says that they must win in order to save the country. That must mean that when the incumbent loses, the country has been saved. Yeah, right.

6. **Beyond their imagination:** The Second Amendment reads: "A well regulated Militia, being necessary to the security of a free State, the right of the people to keep and bear Arms, shall not be infringed." I think the framers of this amendment would have modified it somewhat if they had known that a single shot reload would eventually become an automatic assault weapon capable of firing 300 rounds per minute. Back in the day, mass shootings by one person were unimaginable.

7. Some of our politicians are having trouble rising to the level of mediocrity.

8. We have a great system of governance, and we have come a long way in many respects, including prosperity. But please— we need some stringent guardrails to curtail free speech, AI, dark money, lobbyists, gerrymandering, campaign finance, media platforms, Supreme Court justices . . . yikes!

9. **2020s politics**: Mountains are majestic. They are formidable and beautiful. They have great vertical reach beyond the flat terrain that surrounds them. Metaphorically speaking, one might envision our three branches of government as a snow-capped towering mountain with flowing rivers of legislation that run down to American flatlanders. In recent years, however, many of our politicians have made a molehill out of a mountain.

10. **An irony**: The best hope we have to be rescued from politicians is by other politicians. Thus, the importance of voting.

11. **2025 politics**: It appears that the turbulent times of our political era have exposed severe weaknesses in our governing institutions. Perhaps the political rankle we face today will lead us to a stronger, more vibrant democratic tomorrow. After all, you cannot remedy an aneurysm if you don't know it's there.

12. **The Republican Party versus the Democratic Party**: We should not define one of these parties as the lesser of two evils. That's not civil. However, it would be reasonable to say that one of these parties is the lesser of two bad alternatives.

13. **2023 Op-Ed:** Most of us know that Fox News throws out red meat to its right-wing viewers, and that MSNBC throws out red meat to its left-wing viewers. But it's up to the viewers to recognize the difference between meatballs and sirloin steak. Of course, taste is in the mouth of the diner.

> Perhaps the political rankle we face today will lead us to a stronger, more vibrant democratic tomorrow.

14. **VOTE!** If you choose not to vote, just remember this old Spanish proverb: El que calla concede. (He who is silent concedes the point.)

15. **2025 politics:** It's okay if we're not on the same page, but societal welfare is in jeopardy if we're not even in the same book. However, I remain hopeful.

16. **Some politicians:** We made them more than what they were. But what they became was even less than what they were.

17. **Minority rule problem #1**: North and South Dakota combined have *less than two million people*. California alone *has forty million people*. New York has *twenty million*. These states are justly represented in the House of Representatives by population percentages. However, in the Senate, each state has two senators no matter the size of its population. Thus, a combined sixty million residents of CA and NY have the same number of senators as does North and South Dakota with their combined number of less than two million. That's a *severely-lopsided miscarriage of political representation*, and it's in the Senate, where all the legislation passes or dies, and where all federal judges—including Supreme Court Justices—are confirmed. In 1788, when the Constitution was adopted, the two-senator system worked well because it protected the minority from majority overrule. But that's when population demographics were proportionally reasonable, and there were only 38 states in the Union. Obviously, that is no longer the case. The Constitution did not anticipate densely-populated states from sparsely-populated ones. We now have a system where the needs and wants of the few *unfairly* outweigh the needs and wants of the many. **Bottom line:** *We are becoming a nation without ballast. Our system of governance is unjust, and we are being held hostage by this antiquated system.*

18. **Minority rule problem #2**: Any amendment to the Constitution requires 75% of the states to ratify it. That means that only 13 states out of 50 can block the will of the majority. This disparity becomes a problem when those sparsely populated 13 states represent only 20% (or less) of the American population.

19. **Minority rule problem #3:** The North Atlantic Treaty Organization (NATO) is a defensive military alliance that consists of 30 independent member countries. Any decisions by NATO must be reached by consensus. It takes only one nay vote to scuttle any resolution or proposal by the other 29. I understand the necessity for this international arrangement, but it's minority rule, nonetheless. Perhaps at this point in time, it's the best we can do.

20. **Minority rule problem #4:** The United Nations has the Security Council (UNSC). The Council has 15 members, five of which are permanent members (China, France, Russia, the United Kingdom, and the United States). Any one of these five members can veto any resolution that comes before the Council, even if the other four members and the remaining 190 countries are for it. To be clear: If you have one nay against 194 yeas . . . the resolution fails.

21. How do we stop politicians in power once they have the power to stop us from stopping them? Gerrymandering, dark money, and voter suppression are the three strikes that will retire democracy from the field of play. Oops, I forgot social media's dark side.

22. Some people can't see the forest for the trees; some people can't see the trees for the forest; some politicians can't see either.

23. **2025 politics:** Beware of autocratic tendencies. It was a lesson learned too late in many countries. *It is our responsibility*

to become a clear and present danger to those who have become a clear and present danger.

24. Democracies and the rule of law are a bridge over the turbulent waters of human weakness and misbehavior. However, in totalitarian countries there is no bridge, and everyone who tries to build one ends up in hot water.

25. Because of gerrymandering, dark money, voter suppression, and other such shenanigans, our democratic process has become unbalanced. I think my high school peers had a much more rational approach to the democratic voting process than the so-called grown-up versions we have today. That said, I have confidence in our system of governance, and I believe we will eventually rectify these anomalies. As written in the Preamble: "We the People of the United States, in Order to form a more perfect Union, establish Justice, insure domestic Tranquility, provide for the common defense, promote the general Welfare, and secure the Blessings of Liberty to ourselves and our Posterity, do ordain and establish this Constitution for the United States of America."

26. **Sandy Hook Elementary, CT/Robb Elementary in Uvalde, TX:** When it comes to gun legislation, the so-called adults in Congress continue to take baby steps, while more and more of our babies will no longer be taking steps.

27. I am always amused when politicians accuse each other of playing politics. Of course, they're playing politics . . . what else would they be playing? Football players play football;

tennis players play tennis; politicians play politics. However, unlike sports, the playing field is not fixed; rules of engagement are flimsy at best. Therefore, it behooves the rest of us to sort out the mess. Politics is not a bystander sport. Get off the bench. P.S. -Sometimes I don't practice what I preach.

28. Congresswoman Liz Cheney said the following words at the Ronald Reagan Presidential Library in Simi Valley, CA., on June 29, 2022: "These days, for the most part, men are running the world, and it is really not going that well." I can't argue with that.

29. The "lesser of two evils" is a phrase suggesting that we choose between the lesser of two immoral options. It is frequently used in reference to politicians. When it comes to politics, why can't we be more civil by replacing the expression "the lesser of two evils" with "the lesser of two dislikes"? There's a big difference between being evil and being disliked.

30. Is the opening line of the Preamble to the Constitution, "We the people . . .", the solution to our contentious political discourse, or is it the problem?

31. **Debate:** A bad politician with a good style of delivery will always outshine a good politician with a bad style of delivery. Bells and whistles are the selling points of any good salesperson. Substance, the most important aspect of any debate, seldom prevails over a misleading argument that is strongly delivered.

32. **America:** Free elections may be free, but they're not always fair. Presently (2023), America is not even ranked in the top 20 most democratic countries worldwide. A democracy that has free elections but is stymied by gerrymandering, voter suppression, dark money, unchecked minority rule, and other harmful practices is not truly democratic. Such a system is known as an *illiberal democracy* ("a governing system that hides its nondemocratic practices behind formally democratic institutions and procedures"). The United States will be so classified if these irregularities aren't curbed.

33. **Dinosaurs:** If Republicans can have RINOS (Republicans in name only), why can't Democrats have DINOS (Democrats in name only)?

34. **The Wizard of Oz:** Regrettably, deceitful governance is meted out by politicians with self-serving interests, pulling the levers of power at their disposal. Our moral duty requires that we look behind the curtain.

35. **Double haters:** Before Kamala Harris, when Trump was running against Biden for the presidency, voters who said they were not satisfied with either of the two candidates, were called "double haters." Really? Must we inject such nasty terminology (hate) into the body politic that is already burdened with caustic rhetoric?

36. **Supreme Court Term limits and other guardrails needed:** Why is it that we haven't put into place congressional laws that would mitigate Supreme Court Justices' abuse of power

or, at a minimum, make them accountable for breaking the few laws that do exist? Have we forgotten the long-affirmed wisdom that "power corrupts, and absolute power corrupts absolutely"? To give any one person or group absolute power is to assume they are something other than human.

37. **The ultimate litmus test**: Why do politicians invoke the name of God or Jesus—even if it is feigned—when running for the presidency? The answer is obvious: It's because most Americans believe that anyone running for this high office should be religiously inclined. But our Constitution differs with that misguided notion—Article VI Clause 3: "*... but no religious Test shall ever be required as a Qualification to any Office or public Trust under the United States.*" Accordingly, America is unlikely to prove its democratic chops until an atheist, or someone of another religion, becomes our president.

38. Civil discourse within the body politic has given way to rigor mortis.

39. Not all concepts that emanate from the Constitution are worthy of veneration. But that doesn't disqualify the text from its overall beauty and significance. Even so, we need additional amendments to help bring us into the twenty-first century, lest we render ourselves ineffectual.

40. For various reasons, some people refuse to vote. But everyone votes, like it or not. People shouldn't fool themselves into thinking they're not voting even if they don't cast a ballot. To

rephrase a Christian expression: You can commit the vote of commission, or the vote of omission.

41. **Monetary parallels:** The Mexican cartels have so much money that they literally buy up the authorities that are supposed to arrest and prosecute them—all at the expense of the people. There's a similar process in the United States when billionaires buy up our political leaders and nominees to advance their special interests—all at the expense of the people.

> Not all concepts that emanate from the Constitution are worthy of veneration. But that doesn't disqualify the text from its overall beauty and significance.

42. **Nov. 5, 2024:** Today is our extremely divisive presidential election. Regardless of who wins, I am hopeful that we, as Americans, can regroup after the election is over, without rancor or dispute. Given the situation as I understand it, that rosy outcome is unlikely. But I for one will attempt to live in the spirit of reconciliation. Sometimes music says it best. And so, I offer the 1968 song "Get Together" as a possible conduit

to help reinforce our better angels. It is a song I have cherished these many years. *(Search for "Get Together" by the Youngbloods on YouTube with lyrics.)*

43. A nation divided against itself by allowing unregulated free speech cannot stand in alignment with our better interest. I realize that regulated speech is a contradiction in terms. However, some regulation already exists. For example, "You can't yell fire in a crowded theatre." In like manner, we need regulation on free speech that has some common-sense rules against media outlets that purposely convey false information.

44. **2025 Confirmation hearings:** The Senate is derelict in its duty—regardless of the party in charge—if it only kicks the tires but doesn't check the engine.

45. The difference between what some politicians say and what they believe is like the difference between a measly pothole and the Grand Canyon. That may be an exaggeration, but not by much.

46. You can know too much and see too little; you can know too little and see too much. But if you know too little and see too little, you'll become a politician. (P.S. – We do have a few good politicians.)

47. The Constitution should not be considered sacrosanct. Just like the Bible, it is imperfect and raises unresolved questions. The big C needs a clarifying rewrite.

48. 2025 politics: There is a lesson that Democrats have yet to learn. There are times when personal ethics must be set aside. Trying to play an honest game with a Republican stacked deck is a losing hand at best, and a display of political naiveté at worst. Having said that, I must admit that it's easy for me to criticize from a distance, especially when I'm nowhere near the gaming table, much less in the game.

(*See also Trumpism*)

(Flashback Vol. 1)
Throwing someone "under the bus" is the wrong metaphor when it comes to some politicians. A much, much better political metaphor would be: Throwing someone under the train. There are plenty of reasons why we should throw a politician under the train:

- He got sidetracked.

- He got derailed.

- He was untrained.

- He wasn't on the right track.

- He lost his train of thought.

- He lost track of time.

- He was articulate, but it's not the whistle that pulls the train.

- He fell asleep at the switch.

- He just couldn't make the grade.

- He was a runaway.

- He couldn't stoke up his base.

- His brain was like the caboose, always behind.

- He railroaded the public.

- He didn't have the right ticket.

- He spent too much time drinking in the club car.

- He didn't have enough steam.

- He always got stranded on a siding.

- He was as slick and as crude as the oil car.

- He thought the boxcar was for fist fights.

- He thought the Santa Fe Flyer was an airplane.

- He thought the boiler was for cooking.

- He thought the Super Chief was an Indian.

- He thought the cab car was a taxi.

- He thought the coupling pins were for lovers.

- He thought Home Depot was a railway station.

POTPOURRI

Potpourri

Opinions without facts,
are like trains without tracks.
A problem without answers
is like a floor without dancers.
A dog without a bone
is like a man without a home.
A boy without a girl
is like a nut without a squirrel .
If that last line sounds crazy,
it's because I got lazy.

1. **Boot Hill:** Does anybody know where they buried the cowboys who didn't have boots?

2. The popular expression "Tomorrow is not promised" is only partially correct because the full measure of today isn't either. Just saying . . .

3. **Grasshopper:** In a TV *Kung Fu* episode, the master tells the young student that "one should be nothing, so that one can give everything to others." But I prefer my own thinking on this one: One should be something, so that one can give something to others.

4. It's usually the attitude one takes in the argument that persuades or dissuades.

5. **Health advisory:** It's true that too much salt in your diet is bad for you. It can raise your blood pressure, lead to congestive heart failure, and so forth. Unfortunately, like many of you, I salt my food to the max. Fortunately, I've discovered a way to neutralize the side effects. I counterbalance my salt intake by consuming equal amounts of sugar.

6. Friendship is the oasis that is found in the desert of loneliness.

7. Some people mean well, but they don't know well. Some people know well, but they don't mean well. Some people neither know well nor mean well. Some people both know well and mean well.

8. **Rated R – Adult language:** Sometimes adult language is nothing more than juvenile language imitated by juvenile adults.

9. The only thing worse than a poor loser is a poor winner. Even so, most of us are good sports either way. However,

when the stakes are high, it's never been easy to win humbly or to lose graciously.

10. Can two run-of-the-mill people find happiness running a mill? (This might be another one of my run-of-the-mill memories from a Bazooka Bubble Gum wrapper.)

> "
> It's usually the attitude one takes in the argument that persuades or dissuades.
> "

11. Most people don't go to the dark side; it's the dark side that comes to them.

12. Have you noticed those overhanging signs on the freeway with their drive-safely messages? They can be a dangerous distraction. Traffic seems to slow a bit when drivers going 75 miles per hour try to digest the message. Here's a sign you'll *never* see: "Why are you looking up here? Keep your eyes on the road!"

13. "Enough is enough!" How much longer must we hear this worn-out platitude? It's a trite expression applied across

the board. On and on it goes to the point of nauseum! Please, I don't want to hear that cliché ever again. After all, enough is enough!

14. Almost every rerun movie I see on TV, except for TCM movies, begins with the following acknowledgment: *"This film has been modified from its original version. It has been formatted to fit this screen and edited to run in the time allotted and for content."* But if truth be known, what they're really saying is: This film has been modified from its original version. Segments have been edited out to squeeze in umpteen commercials in the time allotted.

15. We call a horse a horse. We call a donkey a donkey. Why don't we call a horse a horsey and a donkey a donk? Better yet, it would be more consistent if we said horsey and donkey or horse and donk. These are the thoughts that keep me up at night. That, and the theological concept of ex nihilo.

16. There's no better way of starting the day than waking up. That's an assumption.

17. When we were kids we couldn't wait to grow up. Ice cream bars were on my "to get list." But it didn't take us long to discover that no one ever grows up. We simply grow upwards. And in the case of ice cream, we grow outwards (darn). In any case, we've all discovered that growing up is a never-ending process, not a finish.

18. Don't give too much credit to people who do the things that come naturally to them. Giving credit where credit is due is more rightly earned by those who achieve above their pay grade.

> "Sometimes a hero is nothing more than someone who happens to be foolish at the right time."

19. **Mr. Scott, the smartest outlaw:** I've seen many a western movie in my lifetime. It generally happens that posses chasing fugitives usually get their man. That shouldn't happen if the outlaw is thinking. And so it was with Mr. Scott in 1867, who fled a bank robbery with a posse in hot pursuit. It was obvious to him that a bandit on the run should place himself at the right spot, secure his horse, and wait for the posse to show up. That's exactly what Scott did. The sheriff and his

deputies, upon arrival, dismounted, took cover, and began shooting. Obviously, Mr. Scott returned fire with his rifle, but not at the lawmen. Instead, he fired some bullets close to their horses, and the animals scampered off in all directions. Thereafter, he mounted his horse and rode off into the sunset scot-free.

> " The passage of time robs us of our youth, yet simultaneously fills our journey with all kinds of goodies. "

20. **The Hero**: Kudos to those who knowingly jeopardize their own safety on behalf of others. But sometimes a hero is nothing more than someone who happens to be foolish at the right time.

21. Early in his musical career, Brian Wilson of the Beach Boys stumbled on to a simple three-letter word that came to be the foundational formula in some of his hit songs. The word was: "now." For example, in his popular single, "Fun, Fun, Fun," you can hear the word "now" at least 27 times. If Beethoven had only known.

22. Life is an odyssey that begins with hello and ends with goodbye. And nestled in-between those two extremes are countless hellos and goodbyes that mostly come and go like will-o'-the-wisp.

23. Is there any difference between the soul of a stillborn baby and the soul of a senior citizen? The former lacks credits, while the latter is loaded with hard-fought accomplishments and acquired wisdom. It doesn't seem right if it matters. Yet it doesn't seem right if it doesn't.

24. If there's a fly swatter in the room, is the fly on the wall worse off than the fly in the ointment? I'm not sure what that means. It just came to me on the fly.

25. Time is a thief, but a benefactor, nonetheless. The passage of time robs us of our youth, yet simultaneously fills our journey with all kinds of goodies. It's a mixed bag. I'll recycle and modify a different metaphor from Forrest Gump . . . "life is like a box of chocolates," but not altogether absent those jawbreakers.

26. Are you familiar with the 1963 Cinerama movie *It's a Mad, Mad, Mad, Mad World*? If it hadn't been a comedy, the title would be prophetic.

27. I recently tested positive for the flu. Of course, it could have been a false positive. I can't be positive that it wasn't a false positive. But if it was a false positive, then I can rest assured that I was negative. Of that I can be positive.

(Flashback Vol. 1)

Trying to speak rationally to an opinionated person is like trying to sweep the sand of the beach with a toothbrush.

PSYCHOLOGY

Bottoms Up

There are times when you need a psychologist.
There are times when you need a podiatrist.
There are times when you need a neurologist,
but don't ever go near a proctologist.

1. Why should it be so easy bowing down to our lowest impulses, and so hard living up to our highest virtues? It seems like we suffer the same struggle between chocolate and broccoli.

2. From Robert Browning's poem: "Ah, but a man's reach should exceed his grasp, Or what's a heaven for?" But to maximize that "reach," a man's self-image should exceed himself.

3. **Crushed:** Clinical depression immobilizes an individual and, in some cases, this type of melancholia can be life-threatening. It reaches far beyond any bouts of despondency that most of us have experienced at one time or another.

Everyone's been at the bottom of the barrel, but that is still a cut above clinical depression. Those unfortunate souls are not at the bottom of the barrel; they're underneath it!

4. Personal negative thoughts are not personal. Eventually, they form the exoskeleton of our character. They cannot remain hidden indefinitely, despite our behavioral camouflage.

5. History is awash with inaccurate and/or biased information. It is in our best interest to remember that some of our memories are equally tainted; the problem is not knowing which ones are which.

6. The actor: Good or bad, there is never equivalency between a person's persona and their true character. But the bad actor is easily spotted—unless the bad actor is a good actor.

7. The ants go marching one by one: Generally speaking, black ants march in tandem with their co-workers. Aside from the scouts, they travel in lockstep. In contrast, red ants seemingly run amuck, independent of one another; there is no conformity, and that makes their everyday journey unique. Question: Are you a black ant, or a red ant? I think most of us are a combination thereof—it feels good to be a maverick on occasion, but we mostly enjoy comfort and security when we lockstep with like-minded cohorts.

8. **Safety:** We are made safe in the public arena by the rule of law and social mores, but we are never safe from another person's thoughts.

9. Every cloud has a silver lining. That idiom rings true during daylight hours when the rays of light shine through. But during the dark night of the soul there are no silver linings. With fallen spirit, one anxiously awaits the sunrise.

> By virtue of being a normal human being, you're more likely than not to have a skeleton in your closet.

10. Music, laughter, chocolate and friendship are the shock absorbers of life.

11. **Mindscape:** Many people feel they are well adjusted. But what does it mean to be well adjusted? Perhaps we are simply conforming to our societal womb which creates the illusion of being well adjusted. The fact that most people are nationalistic, regardless of their country or beliefs, should give us pause as to whether we are well adjusted or just conforming.

12. We don't like to admit it, but sometimes getting even is the only path to one's peace of mind.

13. **"Love your neighbor as yourself"**: Thank you, Jesus. I always feel good when I do something helpful for someone else. In fact, the good feelings I enjoy are derived from the kindness I practice. I'm also proud in doing so. But then I begin to wonder if the motivation for my kindness is driven by an addiction based on self-gratification rather than altruism. And where is my humility in all of this? It's a psychological conundrum that must rest in the shadows of ambiguity. But one thing is certain: If you're going to have an addiction, this one is primo.

14. Why do we do the things we do? Singular motives are virtually nonexistent. Mixed motives are the norm, and not easily discerned by the individual. I speak from experience.

15. **We are trinitarians**: (1) who people think we are, (2) who we think we are, and (3) who we really are. These three possibilities are never perfectly aligned. However, when they are closely joined, we are well-adjusted individuals. The further apart they are, the more apt we are to be a problem for ourselves and others.

16. **Eye-opener caveat**: They say a one-eyed man would be king in the land of the blind. I don't believe so . . . he's more likely to be ushered into an asylum, if not martyred, based on his abnormal views (pun intended).

17. By virtue of being a normal human being, you're more likely than not to have a skeleton in your closet. To extend that metaphor, there's no excuse for having a house full of them.

18. **Lessons learned:** Some lessons are neutral—they have no positive or negative outcomes. Some lessons are well learned—they help us navigate the future in positive fashion. Some lessons are negative—they are damaging and irreversible.

> If the latter outweighs the former two,
> The result will be a sorrowful you.
> If the former two outweigh the latter,
> That will make you so much gladder.

19. Pseudo-reasoning is a self-serving mechanism that we conveniently employ to justify irrational behavior.

20. I've always been intrigued by false memory, selective memory, confirmation bias, and selective attention. They can lead to diametrical and divisive opinions. We favor our own thoughts because they feel ironclad. But the truth is, we are often off the mark in recall, and we would do well to keep that in mind. Even the old axiom that "seeing is believing" can be misleading. To that end, I offer the following one-minute video for your consideration. Good luck.
(*Search for "selective attention test" on YouTube*)

21. **A cliché with supplement:** "The tough get going when the going gets tough," but the smart stop going when the going's insurmountable.

22. To be disrespected carries a load; to be well-regarded carries a load of its own.

23. **Our conversational bias:** I'm never wrong, except when I am. You're always wrong, except when you're not.

(Flashback Vol. 1)
Am I tired of being someone I am, that others think I'm not, or am I tired of being someone I'm not, that others think I am?

RACE

Black Lives Matter

(This poem from Vol 1)
You are my friends I love you all
But then I wonder if at all,
Our crossing paths and sheer delight
Was brought about by skin of white.

It's very easy you can see
If I were black you'd know not me.
Conversely then I'm sure you'll see,
If you were black I'd know not thee.

Replace your skin by transformation
Allow yourself imagination.
If now your skin did black appear,
Your friends and loves would disappear.
A different train, a different track,
And all because your skin was black.

1. **Blatant racism:** It wasn't the good people of Springfield, Ohio, who amplified the rumor about Haitians eating the neighborhood cats and dogs. That exaggeration came from outsiders. So, let's face it: If Springfield had taken in 10,000 White Ukrainian immigrants instead of Black Haitians, you never would have heard any of that ridiculous gossip. P.S.:— I'm happy to report that all cats, dogs, geese, and ducks have been accounted for.

> "
> Three kinds of people should be treated equally: my kind, your kind, and their kind.
> "

2. **USA:** Guilty by association of ethnicity, color, and race is absent from the white community. But equality will eventually triumph, thanks to the white community that penned the Constitution.

3. **Race and gender:** Three kinds of people should be treated equally: my kind, your kind, and their kind.

4. **Acceptance:** Very few people ever escape the womb of social bias, be it racism, sexism, religion, politics, or nationalism. It is obvious that these narrow-minded attitudes must be overcome if we are to establish a peaceful world order. Strangely enough, I find the lyrics of Disney's "It's a Small World" to be a guiding light, albeit somewhat simplistic. Nevertheless, the tune is catchy, the harmonies are lush, and the lyrics are prime. "Though the mountains divide, and the oceans are wide, it's a small world after all." *(Search for "It's a Small World" [Disney Land Paris] on YouTube)*

> Very few people ever escape the womb of social bias, be it racism, sexism, religion, politics, or nationalism.

(**Flashback Vol. 1**)
"Better late than never:"

- In 1857 the Supreme Court ruled in favor of slavery, and also that African Americans were not citizens.

- In 1896 it declared that segregation was constitutional if facilities were equal.

- In 1920 the right to vote for most women came after the 19th Amendment was ratified, and that right was given to all women by 1928.

- In 1964 the Civil Rights Act outlawed racial and gender discrimination.

- In 2022 the first Black American woman—Ketanji Brown Jackson—was nominated and confirmed to the United States Supreme Court.

RELIGION

A Rule of Thumb for all Believers

(This poem from Vol 1)

Religions play a proper role;
they make our life sublime.
But feelings come and feelings go;
they always fade with time.
So make your move beyond delight;
there's mountains you can climb,
But only if you take the time
to exercise your mind.

1. The road to hell may be paved with good intentions, but the road to heaven is paved with good intentions fulfilled.

2. Righteous indignation provides the perfect excuse for unrighteous behavior.

3. It's difficult for most of us to watch a lioness run down a gazelle, much less observe man's cruelty across the board. One does not see the face of God in Nature's violence, only

in the image of Nature's beauty. Since this division between violence and beauty is an apparent reality, how can God be only on one side of it? However, if God is on both sides, what does that tell us about God? Of course, the Christian answer to this dilemma is to blame man and the so-called Devil for what's gone wrong. But that scapegoat notion is no longer reasonable for me. I'm looking elsewhere, but the answer eludes at every turn.

> The road to hell may be paved with good intentions, but the road to heaven is paved with good intentions fulfilled.

4. Sometimes religious rituals tend to metamorphose into perfunctory repetition.

5. It's a breath of fresh air when a devotee of any faith under-emphasizes man-made doctrinal dogma, while paying closer attention to the love-directed principles that his or her religion offers.

6. **My World Religions class:** *Sati* is an outlawed former Hindu practice in *India whereby a widow allows herself to be*

burned alive on the funeral pyre of her dead husband. Her self-sacrifice supposedly guaranteed a better reincarnation. I gave my college students a quiz and asked them to define sati. Herein are some of their answers. (*Verbatim – nothing has been corrected or changed.*)

- Wife burns her body atop of her husband when he is dead.

- Sati is when a females husband dies, they can burn themselves alive.

- A wife jumps on her husbands funeral fire.

- A woman lays on her husband while he is burning alive.

- Woman says she wants to die with hubby via fire on his spire.

- It's when a husband dies so a wife throws her alive body on his dead burning one.

7. Don't get lost in religiosity; get lost in humanitarianism. The gods will love you for it.

8. To claim that we are created in God's image proves only that we are intelligent enough to be conceited. I could be wrong on this one, but it's an interesting thought, nonetheless.

9. **Eclectic:** I am open to religious insights from various traditions, but I am not open to claims of religious supremacy.

10. Could I trust you to play God for one day? Could you trust yourself to play God for one day? Could you trust me to play God for one day? Could I trust myself to play God for one day? That would be *no* on all counts. Only a fool would think otherwise.

11. If religion is your strong suit, make sure you concentrate on its prime directives of kindness and justice, as opposed to its less impressive directive of fidelity.

12. The acquisition of knowledge strips away the nonessential beliefs of one's spiritual path. Continued intellectual enhancement chips away at the hardcore center of blind faith, i.e., the faith I started out with as a youngster. Further learning creates a custom-made journey that may, or may not, satisfy the seeker's quest. It's not for everyone.

13. Is there a God? That's a profound question. More importantly, why is it that life isn't fair—God or no God? Some would argue that man is responsible for this dilemma. Give me a break!

14. One day, in my collegiate World Religions class, I asked my college students if anyone knew how the Buddha died. A young man raised his hand and asked: "Was it a car accident?"

15. It is gratifying to have religious faith. But it's also liberating not feeling like one must have it to avoid nasty consequences. At that point, faith becomes a choice, not a mandate. I leave that to your interpretation.

16. Religion is not the problem . . . religionism is.

17. One man's religion is another man's falsehood.

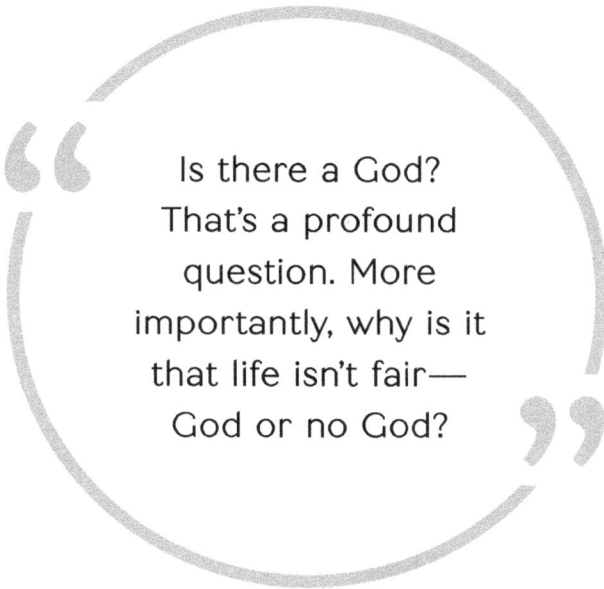

> Is there a God?
> That's a profound
> question. More
> importantly, why is it
> that life isn't fair—
> God or no God?

18. **The best of both worlds:** Religion is like a beach umbrella that blocks out the blazing sun and protects you against serious sunburn. However, to soak up the full beach experience, one needs to step out from underneath that religious shield. But when you do, be sure to have plenty of sunscreen on hand. The brand I recommend is called "Open-Mindedness" SPF 70. And for those of you who have never rested under the religious umbrella, you might find it refreshing to get out of the scorching sun for a change.

19. If you spend more time in a house of worship than the everyday battlefield of human need, then you're in the wrong house of worship.

20. **Wait for it**:

Prehistoric beliefs – Nature worship, ancestor worship, animism, totemism, shamanism, etc.

3500 BC – Sumerian beliefs

2500 BC – Hinduism beliefs

2000 BC – Jewish beliefs

1800 BC – Mayan beliefs

1500 BC to 500 AD – Greco-Roman beliefs (mystery religions)

1300 BC – Aztec beliefs

500s BC – Buddhism, Jainism, Taoism, Confucianism beliefs

33 AD – Christian beliefs

622 AD – Islamic beliefs

1400s AD – Sikhism beliefs

1500s AD – Unitarian beliefs

1600s AD – Deism beliefs

1700s AD – Pantheism beliefs

1800s AD – Panentheism beliefs, Mormon beliefs, Baha'i beliefs

1900s AD – Wicca beliefs, Scientology beliefs

5000s AD – ?

Point: *We may think we choose our beliefs; but the beliefs of our time and place choose us* (if you get my drift).

21. **Theological musing:** What does it mean to die young—the glass half-full, the tank not filled—long before life experience and acquired wisdom have shaped the final product on the Potter's wheel?

> We may think we choose our beliefs; but the beliefs of our time and place choose us.

22. **World Religions:** How much stock should an individual place in a belief system that is more than 2000 (Christianity) or 4000 (Hinduism) years old? Some concepts are obviously obsolete. But they all have precious metals therein; the trick is knowing the difference between gold and fool's gold.

23. **Tongue-in-cheek:** To say that man is created in the image of God is somewhat akin to saying that a donkey is created in the image of man.

24. Is there a God? I now consider this to be a minor question. I'm not arguing against belief in God; that's a personal matter left to the individual. But I believe our real concern should focus more on the human condition. I can't help but believe that being attentive to God should be secondary to human problem-solving.

25. When it comes to religion, is it better to be an antiquated relic, or a misguided modernist? You're right . . . a multiplicity of options between these two extremes are at one's disposal.

26. Religion is the ultimate rabbit hole. But it's a good place to be if you're a rabbit, and the carrot cakes are delicious. That metaphor is not meant to be disparaging. I've gone down that rabbit hole a few times in my life and have found it to be comforting. However, these days I prefer to be above ground; the view is much clearer from this vantage point, at least for me (although I do miss the cakes).

27. Can I be dedicated to God without being dedicated to God's purposes? Can I be dedicated to God's purposes without being dedicated to God? Does it make a difference in either case? Of course, most would say that being committed to both would be ideal. But that doesn't answer my questions.

28. It's important to know the difference between a *religious scholar of religion* and a *nonreligious scholar of religion*. A religious scholar of religion tends to interpret historical facts through the prism of faith and is thereby prone to biased conclusions. A nonreligious scholar of religion is more likely to render an objective judgment without the overlay of religious spin. The right or wrong of each approach is left to the individual. *Note: nonreligious does not mean antireligious.*

29. Religion has a dark side, no denying. But that is simply because people have a dark side, and religions are comprised of people. What else would you expect? Importantly, the inverse of that dark side is notable.

30. I'm always a little wary about people who claim to know the will of God, talk to God, or imagine divine intervention at every turn. The following line from the 1946 movie, *Sister Kenny* (played by Rosalind Russell), sums it up nicely: "It's not the things we don't know that get us in trouble; it's the things we do know that just ain't so."

31. Religions don't own the concepts of love and forgiveness, but they far and away lead the pack.

32. In our birth culture, there is always a primary religion of choice. In the United States, it's Christianity; in India, it's Hinduism; in Japan, it's Shinto and Buddhism; in Saudi Arabia, it's Islam, and so forth. Within geographical boundaries, familiarity doesn't breed contempt; it breeds conformity. Conformity immunizes many believers against any rational

analysis of their faith-based convictions and normalizes the most ludicrous of their beliefs. That is why followers of a different stripe can always spot the other camp's absurdities while not recognizing their own.

33. **Price of admission**: Regardless of what we've heard, there is no such thing as unconditional love, and certainly not from the gods of any religion.

> "If religion is your strong suit, make sure you concentrate on its prime directives of kindness and justice, as opposed to its less impressive directive of fidelity."

34. Religion, and religious acts, are neither regulated by the state, nor the federal government, and the clergy are the only unregulated professional group in America. Self-imposed guardrails are usually inadequate. Although the separation of

church and state is a good thing, we need to be aware that religious freedom can, and has, led to negative consequences. A few commonsense regulations would be advisable.

35. **Question:** When it comes to religion and politics, certitude is amplified to the tenth power, and most people remain stuck in their fortified silos. Why do you think that is?

36. Even if the gods should exist, we should never spend our time worshiping them at the expense of addressing the human condition. I earnestly believe that the gods would have us concentrate on the latter rather than the former.

37. The major religions of the world are successful because they provide hypothetical signposts to a theoretical afterlife. In addition, they provide easy, soothing, so-called answers to unanswerable questions. Right or wrong, they are the rudders "On the Good Ship Lollipop."

38. To kneel before the gods has been humanity's greatest codependent pastime. The practice has merit despite some negative outcomes. Nevertheless, in due course, our human evolution will demand a weaning process.

39. Religion is quicksand. Once you're in it, the result can be a progressive loss of rational thought. Thankfully, not all believers fall into that category.

40. Because of my formal education, I know what I know about religion, and that troubles me. But the subject matter

is teeming with mystery. So, to exclude all religious under-pinnings on the basis of what I know, or don't know, would be naïve .

41. **Metamorphose**: Initially, religions develop slowly, but they never remain pristine. Over time, they are redeveloped. The latter is usually quite different than its original. The degree of embellishment or modification varies. However, who's to say whether that transformation is, or is not, for the better? The beauty of the spiritual realm is in the eye of the beholder, and in the ear of the listener.

(Flashback Vol. 1)
I am put-off by religious authoritarianism, not by religious opinions that differ from mine.

ROMANCE

CHEERS

(This poem from Vo1 1)

A champagne lady with beauty and grace
Is not gonna fall for a beer-looking face.
I've always had trouble and suffered fatigue,
When chasing a woman outside of my league.

The champagne lady didn't give me a chance,
Not even a smile, not even a dance.
And when I was near her I felt out of place,
You can chalk it all up to this beer-looking face.

The years passing by took her fizz and her bubble,
And as it turned out she was nothing but trouble.
Champagne is a temptress that's always the case,
But I rescued myself with this beer-looking face.

1. Love at first sight is magical. Love at last sight can be forever haunting.

2. **"Love Potion #9"**: If you have never tasted the intoxicating elixir of romantic love, then you have missed out on a whole lot of misery. On the other hand, stay away from it altogether if you're allergic to euphoria. It's a paradox.

3. **Sex and all good things considered:** The moment in which we live is more highly prized if one recognizes that consistency and stability are short-lived.

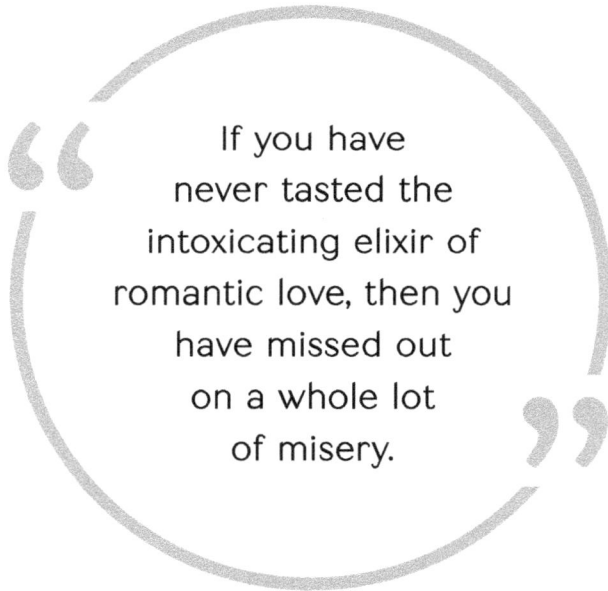

> If you have never tasted the intoxicating elixir of romantic love, then you have missed out on a whole lot of misery.

4. You probably remember the first time you fell in love. As for me, it was like falling out of a tree. It must have been a California redwood because I hit the ground pretty hard.

5. Today's entertainment media leaves little to the imagination when it comes to lovemaking. In contrast, the old Hollywood movies ignited one's imagination without graphic depiction. For example, when lovers kissed on the silver screen, their passion was measured. Film directors never emphasized desire to the max because they instinctively knew that less was better than more. They were right. Few of us enjoy seeing two lovers trying to eat each other's tonsils.

6. The enigmatic nature of love is that we can be accepted despite our shortcomings, and then be rejected for the same reasons when the pixie dust settles.

7. Love, by its very nature, will demand a good measure of grief. Grief, by its very nature, will depend on the measure of love.

> The enigmatic nature of love is that we can be accepted despite our shortcomings, and then be rejected for the same reasons when the pixie dust settles.

8. People often say, "Hope for the best, prepare for the worst." There are times when you cannot prepare for the worst—you

can only anticipate the worst. It's a distinction worth noting. As one example, you can anticipate a broken heart, but you cannot prepare for one.

9. The exhilarating high in a teenage crush is painfully matched by its inevitable decline.

(Flashback Vol. 1)
Whoever it was that said, "The anticipation is greater than the realization," must have been celibate.

SCIENCE

Jimmy O'Shea

Is Jimmy O'Shea okay?
Can Jimmy come out and play?
He got sick as a dog
when he visited Prague.
Is Jimmy O'Shea okay?

We're delighted and happy to say,
that Jimmy can come out and play.
We made an alliance
and followed the science,
so Jimmy O'Shea is okay.

If you want to be healthy today,
take a lesson from Jimmy O'Shea.
Embrace modern science,
with faithful reliance,
it is certainly better that way.

1. It's the social and physical sciences that have forced religions to reframe their beliefs, not vice versa.

2. A large segment of our society is anti-science, anti-college education, and anti-intellectualism. I suggest that these individuals have a mindset not compatible with logic or good judgment

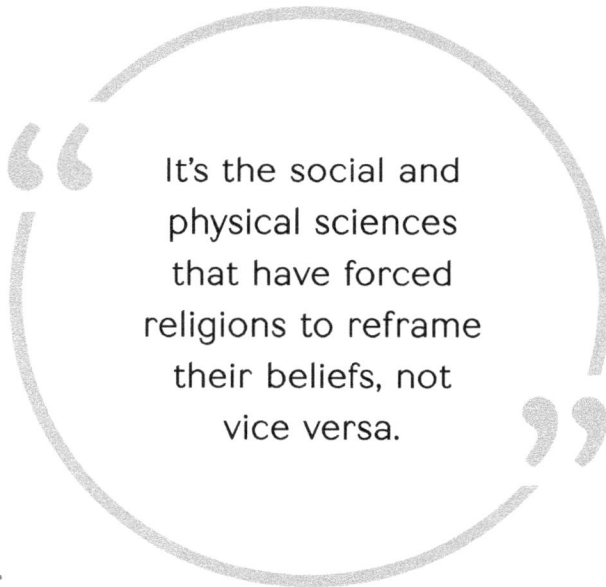

> " It's the social and physical sciences that have forced religions to reframe their beliefs, not vice versa. "

3. We can learn from science that a failed experiment is a form of progress.

4. It seems that people must be the victims of brutality before they feel and understand the rage of retribution. But the

question arises: Where is the dividing line between justified retribution and unwarranted revenge? The *rational answer* to that question should not be made by the wounded heart.

5. The fossil record tells us that our prehistoric 400cc brains have evolved into our present 1300cc brains (that process of IQ enhancement will continue). Consequently, that is proof positive that the more intellectual we become, the more and more God recedes into the background. We've come a long way since worshipping the sun god. This raises a question: Is man's supercharged intelligence God's created problem, even as AI is man's created problem?

6. Religion gives the comforting impression of progression towards truth, and that may be the case. Science also gives the comforting impression of progression towards truth, *and that is the case.*

7. **Outrunning the science:** Aside from accidental death and other premature variables, our date of birth will determine the parameters of our longevity based on the prevailing science of our time. In other words, if I had not been born during the scientific age of aortic valve replacement, I would have died decades ago. No such luck for my ancestors who had this genetic abnormality. But eventually, *we outrun the science.* That is, all of us will die prior to a scientific breakthrough that would have saved us. It's always the case that people either die shortly before, or shortly after, scientific breakthroughs occur, i.e., insulin, antibiotics, etc. So, it's not only survival of the fittest, but survival of the luckiest.

8. **Good news:** I just heard from a friend of mine who keeps up with the latest medical science. Her sources declare that if a person can live to be 105, they have a good chance of living to be 106.

9. **Science and religion:** Scientists, as scientists, have no privileged access to what happens in the supernatural realm; they have access only to what happens in this, our natural world. Whether they deny or accept a theistic view, they do so, not in their capacity as scientists but in their capacity as believers or nonbelievers. *Science is a neutral discipline; it neither affirms nor denies the spiritual realm. It is essential for us to distinguish the difference between the scientific method and a scientist's personal notions.*

10. Science derails itself when it becomes dogmatic, and that's especially true of religion.

11. **Astrobiology:** The significance of our species may be overvalued. That possibility is based on the unawareness most people have of the billion-timeline continuum that predates, and will postdate, our existence. Not unlike the dinosaurs that went extinct 65 million years ago, it's the never-ending parade of here today and gone tomorrow. Of course, the religions of the world suggest a valued afterlife of some sort. Even a smidgen of truth in that last sentence would be a Godsend.

12. Is humanity the first breakthrough wonder of natural evolution, or the first blunder? The jury is still out on this one, but I'm pulling for the former.

13. **A moving target**: It is scientifically true that we, as a species, are in the process of development. The evolutionary difference between what we were in yesteryear, what we are today, and what we'll be in future years, is astonishing. Therefore, I have concluded that man is not fully developed in God's image. Not yet anyway. I think we are more like a Lego set that God is trying to piece together in His image. Judging from the human condition and the slow process of evolution, God is either looking for some missing pieces or taking a long coffee break.

> Science is a neutral discipline; it neither affirms nor denies the spiritual realm. It is essential for us to distinguish the difference between the scientific method and a scientist's personal notions.

14. I'm in favor of enhancing our genetic codes. If we ignore or reject this newly discovered potential, we have little chance of escaping animalistic behavior. Of course, I would vote to retain our libidos.

15. The time in which we live is our prison. It's a lifetime sentence without judge and jury. It has no bars, guards, or wardens. Aside from dying, escape is impossible, and The Time Machine is only a sci-fi movie. Of course, there's always cryogenics. However, we elderly have enough trouble keeping up with the ever-evolving technology of our own time, let alone waking up in a futuristic society where computers and cell phones are museum pieces, and IQ norms have risen. That would be like bringing a Neanderthal into our own space. Then again, maybe future science could implant a brain-chip that would bring us up to speed in a nanosecond. Hmm . . .

16. There was a time when people could only dream of having protection against smallpox, measles, polio, and all manner of deadly infection (e.g., the bubonic plague). Millions suffered as they prayed to their gods for relief, but the scourge of death raged on. Then came the scientific breakthroughs of immunizations. The masses flocked to those lifesaving vaccinations. Today, we are smarter because we can *decide not to take them.* Wait, what?

(Flashback Vol. 1)

Bath and bodily functions: According to the California Academy of Sciences, there are an estimated 6.5 million species found on land, and 2.2 million dwelling in the oceans. But I think humans carry an inconvenient handicap. They are the only creatures on the planet that have garments to remove before doing what comes naturally.

SOCIAL MEDIA

(This paragraph from Vol 1)
It seems that the Internet is both a godsend and a "devil-send." This Orwellian cosmic battle has yet to be determined. On the one hand, too many sources of truth and rational thought have become blurred by self-serving individuals of every stripe who peddle outright lies, half-truths, and who spew out hatred, bigotry and bullying online. On the other hand, the wealth and availability of fingertip information is unprecedented in human history.

1. **Deepfake (synthetic media):** The old saying "Seeing is believing" was a reasonable guideline. Deepfake has shattered that assumption. We must now contend with a new catch-phrase: Seeing is deceiving.

2. Any person who slavishly follows social media platforms is usually a person who is simultaneously guided and misguided but is unable to tell the difference.

3. **Media fallout:** If we fail to redefine the freedom of speech in the digital age, the repercussions will be costly? You can bet on it.

4. The fog of war cannot rival the fog of social media!

5. **Warning:** One of the consequences of AI could be to diminish human creativity. If AI has the potential to outdo human artists, musicians, poets, actors, screenwriters, writers of all genres, who will aspire to master these creative spheres? There go my Ernie-isms.

6. Back in the mid twentieth century, when I was a teenager, there was a jest going around that made us smile. It went like this: "My mind is made up. Don't confuse me with the facts." (That quote is a variation from Plato's quip: "I'm trying to think. Don't confuse me with facts.") Of course, the question for us today is, how do we discern the facts? Given the misinformation and disinformation of social media platforms, not to mention the misuse of AI, it will be much more difficult to discern truth from untruth. *Vet your sources.*

7. **2024:** On Friday, July 12, computers and tech systems crashed worldwide. The outage disrupted airports, hospitals, businesses, you name it. Evidently, the Cyber firm, Crowd-Strike, forgot to heed Ernie-ism #1: "The quality of life is predicated on the decisions made prior to the crises."

8. People want to hear back the same falsehoods they have been conditioned to believe are true by the so-called trustworthy

TV networks (let alone the other social media platforms) that present them as such. Thereafter, these carnival barkers can no longer change the trumped-up stories they have instilled in their listeners as unquestionable truths, for fear of losing their audience and ratings. Therefore, they must continue to embrace and project the lies they have spewed out to their viewers (conspiracy theories, stolen elections, a propped-up Putin, etc.). The result is a deluded viewership, a misinformed electorate, and "A house divided against . . . ." Uh-oh.

> "It seems that the Internet is both a godsend and a "devil-send." This Orwellian cosmic battle has yet to be determined."

9. **Freedom of speech:** FIRE! We all know that you can't yell fire in a crowded theatre. That is not protected free speech under the First Amendment of the Constitution. Certain common-sense rules do apply. Therefore, as a possible remedy against the inflammatory disinformation of certain social media outlets, I propose that we visualize the surrounding coastlines and borders of the USA as the framing perimeters of a colossal theater and regulate accordingly?

10. **Twitter (X):** Aside from our personal experience, all knowledge we receive from others is hearsay knowledge, that is to say, secondhand knowledge (be it written, verbal, or digital). Unfortunately, it seems that our mental netting is so porous that we allow almost anything to pass through without scrutiny.

11. The human tendency to be gullible stands in contrast to those very few individuals who scrutinize and filter-out misinformation, propaganda, conspiracy, and disinformation.

(Flashback Vol. 1)
Sometimes social media platforms provide followers with a speedway to an off-ramp that takes them directly to the cross streets of Misinformation and Disinformation.

SPORTS

Aspiration

I tried out for football in high school.
I dreamed of the glory since preschool.
My forte was playing on offense.
My weakness apparent on defense.
I never did learn how to tackle.
When I tried I was flayed like a mackerel.

I thought I did well when I ran,
until I got knocked on my can.
I gave it my best with some hustle.
I just didn't have enough muscle.

The moral reveals limitation,
assessment and good correlation.
You'll suffer the pain and fatigue,
if you wander outside of your league.

1. **Football (2022):** I've noticed lately that ads have crept onto the playing field. What was once an unbroken solid 100 yards of green grass has been plastered with intrusive ads or bowl names—some of them ten yards wide in the middle of the field. It's distracting and annoying to see these blatant advertisements on the gridiron. This is just another First-World problem I must endure.

2. A typical redundant pregame, halftime, postgame interview with a coach or player:
Interviewer: Blah blah, blah, blah blah.
Coach/player: Blah, blah, blah, blah blah.

3. **Pet peeve:** It's hard not to notice that football and baseball players have the uncouth habit of spitting all over the playing field. What is it with these guys? Spitting on national TV is bad-mannered, and it echoes down to the young boys trying to mimic their adult heroes. It's a mindless practice that stems from "monkey see, monkey do." And it's totally unnecessary. If that were not so, indoor basketball would be one heck of a slippery mess.

4. **Bad cliché:** "If you can't beat them, join them." Oh, you mean like golf's PGA merger with Saudi Arabia's backed LIV Golf?

5. **Bambi Meets Godzilla:** Almost every sporting event has an underdog. If we don't have a vested interest, we tend to favor the weaker opponent, especially if they have little chance of winning. We draw satisfaction if the results differ from

expectation. The following one-minute video may, or may not, serve that purpose. P.S. – For your enjoyment, pay attention to the credits before and after the main part of this video. *(Search for Bambi Meets Godzilla [1969] on You Tube.)*

6. **Tom Brady & Serena Williams:** Everyone eventually loses. But losing at the finish is not losing. It's the track record that counts.

7. The real reason football players wear a helmet and shoulder pads is because every time one of them recovers a fumble, intercepts a pass, kicks a winning field goal, or makes a touchdown, his teammates pummel him with congratulatory whacks to the head and body.

8. What's with all this 24-hr pregame buildup of the Super Bowl, and all the star-studded entertainment that goes with it? Is the Super Bowl becoming an afterthought? I don't think so, but jeez.

9. **Super Bowl 2025:** I turned the TV on about a half hour before game time and was fortunate to hear Lady Gaga sing a song that brought tears to my eyes. She performed in the middle of the street in New Orleans. She was surrounded by celebs and everyday people. Her performance was inspirational. "Hold My Hand" was a song of hope and support, meted out in the painful memories of the murderous pickup truck attack earlier that year that killed fifteen people, and injured at least fifty-seven others. I offer two videos for your perusal. The first one records her actual performance in New

Orleans. For sure, that is the one you want to see. You may not catch all the lyrics (especially at the beginning), but you can't miss the power and essence of this song as it progresses to a resonating crescendo. The second is her recording of the song with lyrics (worth your time). *(Search for "Hold My Hand" Super Bowl LIX 2025. Also, "Hold My Hand" [Lyrics) on YouTube)*

10. The terms hunting and fishing are euphemisms for killing.

11. If you're a sore loser, you've lost twice. If you're a good sport when winning, you've won twice. As hard as it is to be a good loser, sometimes it's more difficult to be a gracious winner.

(Flashback Vol. 1)

Just prior to the start of a college football game between Texas and USC, I saw players on both sides of the field taking a knee with head bowed in solemn prayer. Aside from throwing Gatorade on the winning coach, this is the silliest, most nonsensical act performed by young athletes. They must be stupid, uninformed, or theologically discombobulated; praying on the gridiron is a waste of time. Don't these idiots know that God doesn't take sides unless Notre Dame is on the field?

TRUMPISM

"The emperor has no clothes."
Power unveils, and absolute power unveils absolutely.

1. The power of a charismatic and bombastic personality should not take precedence over the strength of character. Unfortunately, in our society it often does.

2. **Equivalency**: The law sees no difference between a VIP and a less privileged person. Yeah, right!

3. Why does it take so many red flags for us to realize that our democracy is in jeopardy? After all, it doesn't take more than one canary in the coal mine to recognize a clear and present danger. What's that you say? "It can't happen here." Gosh, where have we heard that before?

4. **Presidential Op-Ed (October 28, 2024)**: I quote from a former Ernie-ism to address the problem of American misogyny,

with added comment on other issues. "Since 1950, dozens of countries have elected or appointed women as heads of state and government—for example: Mongolia, India, China, Israel, Argentina, United Kingdom, Portugal, Bolivia, Iceland, France, Poland, Canada, New Zealand, South Korea, Peru, Germany, South Africa, Australia, Denmark, Jamaica, Greece, Taiwan, Singapore, Romania, Vietnam, Switzerland, Austria, etc., etc., etc." *Frankly, manhood and misogyny are incompatible.* Unfortunately, American misogyny is an aberration that will be exacerbated by the Donald Trump specter. That specter also undermines the rule of law, undermines our democratic institutions, creates chaos in the national fabric, threatens international security as well as our own, threatens access to reproductive rights, violates our moral and ethical norms, and threatens our US economy that is presently the envy of the world, to name a few.

5. **2024 Secret Service miscues**: Sometimes complacency and carelessness are the byproducts of long-standing tranquility.

6. **Feb. 6, 2025**: Is the new Trump administration akin to Wyatt Earp cleaning up Tombstone, or is it more like the Joker trying to take over Gotham City? It feels more like the latter, but time will tell.

7 **Presidential immunity**: Since jr. high school, we have all heard the truism that "Power corrupts, and absolute power corrupts absolutely." So, why is it that the 2024 right-wing Supreme Court justices ignored this accepted wisdom by granting presidential immunity? This gives the president a

good measure of absolute power, and we know where that leads. The conservative justices have argued that hypotheticals are unlikely and make rulings as if those hypotheticals don't exist. They do. The Court disregards the proverbial saying that sometimes "Truth is stranger than fiction." Presidential immunity places the president above the law and opens the door for a presidential autocrat. Eventually, this ruling will be overturned; it cannot stand the test of time.

8. Is it more important for one's life to be interesting, or to be productive? Well, that depends on what makes it interesting and what makes it productive. The ideal would be both, but that's not always the case. As one example, being named Person of the Year on *Time* magazine's cover may be appropriate for someone who is interesting but not necessarily productive.

9. **Partisan**: Republican Senator Mitt Romney voted to impeach Donald J. Trump in 2020. Good for him. But what is troubling to note is that no US senator of any party—since the formation of Congress—had ever voted to impeach one of its own. For this historic act, he received the yearly John F. Kennedy Profile in Courage Award. As for the others, someone needs to create an "Impeachment Profile in Cowardice Award." Make that plural (Awards).

10. Is the power of the people more powerful than the people in power, or is it the other way around? The 2026 midterm elections may provide valuable insights.

11. In the long run, ignorance never trumps knowledge, but it takes a hell of a toll, nonetheless.

12. One night I dreamed that I had died and gone to Heaven. Saint Peter greeted me at the Pearly Gates. He offered to show me around the celestial grounds. Not unlike Disneyland, Heaven was divided into different theme parks. I didn't see any "Pirates of the Caribbean," but we did come across a theme area called "Heavenly Pastimes." We entered a long hallway leading to many rooms where angels were involved in various activities. As we passed the first room, one could hear the numerous angels singing their favorite hymns. Another room featured angels that had an interest in painting, and their portraits were beautiful. Every room we passed had plenty of angels engaged in some form of favored activity. We finally came to a room that was filled with boisterous laughter. I couldn't help but wonder what all the excitement was about. "Why are these angels laughing so hard?" I asked inquisitively. St. Peter answered: "This is the Reading Room and they're browsing through some of Trump's speeches."

13. A man who is full of himself is truly empty.

(Flashback Vol. I)
If people finally discover that the emperor has no clothes, it may not matter. The absence of clothing has no meaning if we find ourselves in a political nudist colony—stripped, as it were, from our basic democratic values, norms, and institutions.

TRUTH/REALITY

A Penny for Your Thoughts

(This poem from Vol 1)

As sure as the night will follow the day,
You can't agree with all that I say.
Well I don't mind, I think that's good,
For we all think as right we should.
If we all thought the very same way,
We'd never see a better day.
The tree of knowledge bears no fruit,
If all we do is follow suit.

1. Truth, by definition, does not have opposing viewpoints. People can voice different opinions about what they think is true, but opinion, or disagreement, never changes reality. For example, there was a time when we thought smoking was benign. Now we know better. *But it wasn't the truth that changed; it was our perception of what we thought was the truth that changed.* It never was true that smoking was benign. For sure, people can disagree with the obvious or deny the obvious. The Flat Earth Society still argues that the world is flat. Such

people are incorrigible, and no amount of logic or factual data will persuade otherwise.

2. It is without a doubt that "no one corners the market on truth." But in our thinking, that idiom doesn't translate into equivalency. Each of us believes we have cornered the better part of it and believe ourselves to be the supermarket of all things rational.

> " People can voice different opinions about what they think is true, but opinion, or disagreement, never changes reality. "

3. Like a buoyant cork placed at the depths of the sunless ocean floor, there is nothing that can stop the truth from rising toward the light of day.

4. Our society takes the position that *truth is of ultimate importance* and should be highly prized. That's why we put people

under oath. Lying under oath is a crime. However, by establishing this separate category (oath), we have inadvertently cut the baby in half. If truth is so vital, why do we have to establish such a division? It's almost like telling people it's okay to lie if they're not under oath. *On matters of importance,* the requirement for speaking the truth should be a universal mandate under penalty of law. No special oath declaration should be necessary to make it so.

5. **Worldviews**: We are all detached from reality. It's not a matter of if; it's a matter of degree. Forget the writing on the wall. Many Earthlings can't even see the Earth because they're on the backside of the Moon.

6. You may ask me: Do I selectively highlight the facts that support my preconceived beliefs, or do I look at the facts wholistically in the pursuit of honest inquiry? You may ask, but I'm taking the Fifth on this one.

7. **The primary principle**: Aside from the normal commitments that one makes to human endeavors and relationships, I believe that our ultimate commitment must be to the pursuit of truth. Our final allegiance should not be to a sacred text, a religion, a divine prophet, a political leader, or a noble cause. Those are secondary. Seeking the truth is primary. That does not begin with the assumption that one already possesses the truth, but that one seeks the truth. And if a thousand sacred beliefs are swamped in its revelation, we are the better for it, nonetheless. Aside from love, truth is the hinge on which all else hangs.

8. Reality is my favorite playground, but not always my favorite comfort zone.

9. Whenever I read or hear something, even if I feel the media feed is honest, I try not to assume that what I'm reading or hearing is the truth. Instead, I conclude that I'm absorbing someone else's version of the truth (which may, or may not, be accurate). Similarly, I must remind myself that what I hold to be true is not the absolute truth, only my version of it.

> "
> Time, curiosity, ingenuity, logic, and the scientific method are the filters that separate truth from falsity, innovation from stagnation.
> "

10. I think I know everything I need to know. However, I could be wrong since I don't know everything there is to know.

11. I wish the media would stop using the phrase alternative facts, or alternative reality, even though most of us know what's implied. But that language could mislead. There's no such thing as an alternative reality, even in the field of quantum mechanics. Reality is a state of things as they exist. The

word "alternative" is defined as offering another possibility. There cannot be another possibility in the face of actuality (assuming we know the actual). Therefore, there can only be a choice between reality and pseudo reality, not alternative reality, or facts and pseudo facts, not alternative facts.

12. Perspective is not always reality. When one faces reality—things as they really are, and not as we wish them to be—that's when life becomes a challenge because sometimes the truth is hard to face. Take heart, you're not alone.

13. All we know is what we've been told. But how do we know that's the rock-bottom truth? Well, we rely on the expertise of those who know more than we do, which in themselves are not foolproof. Nevertheless, if we lack standards of agreement about what is trustworthy, it will lead us directly to harmful division and misgovernment.

> Aside from love, truth is the hinge on which all else hangs.

14. "Truth is stranger than fiction." This proverb tells us that real life is sometimes filled with unlikely absurd or bizarre

events. That may explain our existence, and possibly that of the entire universe, despite my hope to the contrary.

15. Time, curiosity, ingenuity, logic, and the scientific method are the filters that separate truth from falsity, innovation from stagnation.

(Flashback Vol. 1)
Perception is not reality; perception is what people think reality is.

WAR

Russia/Ukraine

It's the agony that smothers,
With the loss of sons and brothers.
It's the hand of hate that slaughters,
And the rape of wives and daughters.
It's the loss of dads and mothers,
And the pain of all the others.

When you kill them by attrition,
And you force them to submission,
They will not become compliant,
They will always be defiant.

When you brutalize a nation,
With such deadly confrontation,
Maybe land is what you're seeking,
But it's hatred you'll be reaping.

War is not a simple matter,
And there's always too much chatter.
What we need is a Mandela,
Or a Gandhi loving fella.

> Peace can never be one-sided,
> Lest the gesture be derided.
> When agreement is decided,
> It is lost if not abided.

1. Words from a Ukrainian Mother: "War sends the son of a mother to kill the son of another."

2. 2023: People all over the world are protesting Israel's invasion of the Gaza Strip, based on humanitarian concerns for innocent Palestinians. I too am appalled by the carnage. Killing thousands of civilians is not the path to a lasting peace. But we need to remind ourselves that it's easy to express righteous indignation when it's not our country that was invaded, and it wasn't our people who got slaughtered, or taken as hostages (exceptions noted). Under those circumstances, no group, no tribe, no clan, no country, has ever turned the other cheek. I'm not saying that's right. I'm just saying that people are righteously indignant until the shoe is on the other foot.

3. The Holocaust, wars, and medieval witch hunts: The *common man* is never so monstrous as when he is granted permission to be inhuman by a higher authority.

4. Irony: There were over a million casualties in the Mexican Revolution (1910-1920). My grandparents escaped that bloody war by crossing the US border in 1916 with my six-month-old mother. That was a seminal moment that forever changed the trajectory of my mother's life. It is one of the main factors that made my life possible twenty-four years later when she married my dad. Thank God for the Mexican Revolution. Wait, what?

5. **Military strategy**: I don't buy into the MAD (mutual assured destruction) philosophy that politicians claim will prevent a nuclear disaster from annihilating everyone. What could possibly go wrong? The acronym itself conveys an ironic MADness.

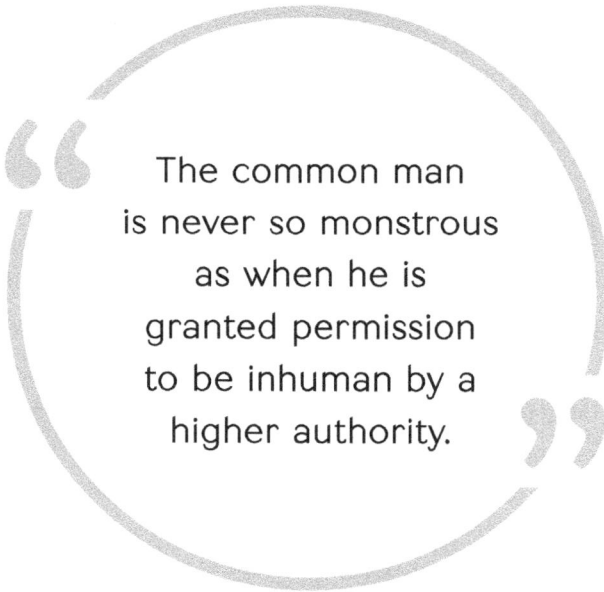

> "The common man
> is never so monstrous
> as when he is
> granted permission
> to be inhuman by a
> higher authority."

6. WWI (estimated 10 million killed), was once called "The War to End All Wars." Unfortunately, history has proved otherwise, and weapons of mass destruction continue to remind us of catastrophic possibilities. At the present time—2024—nine countries have nukes: United States, Russia, United Kingdom, France, China, India, Pakistan, Israel, and North

Korea (Iran is in the wings). Oops, make those ten countries: The dictator Alexander Lukashenko from Belarus got some from Putin/Russia last year. Ugh.

> "
> The best way to curtail war and mass immigration on planet Earth is through the globalization of prosperity.
> "

7. **War, racism, antisemitism, homelessness, etc.:** We all have the luxury of opinions, but we do not live inside of another person's nightmare. Lacking their experience, we grapple with different perspectives and emotions, and that makes our assessments suspect.

8. **"You maniacs! You blew it up! Ah, damn you! God damn you all to hell!"** This emotive quote comes from the 1968 film *Planet of the Apes*, when the astronaut George Taylor (played by Charlton Heston) sees the ruins of the Statue of Liberty on the beach, and realizes he is back on Earth—an Earth that has been devastated by nuclear war. This thematic scenario could be prophetic. However, some people think we're too smart to make that mistake. But we humans repeatedly

prove, even when we're not stupid, that we are inclined to do dumb things.

9. The best way to curtail war and mass immigration on planet Earth is through the globalization of prosperity.

10. **War:** It takes two to tangle, and countless atrocities before it gets untangled.

11. **The American Civil War:** It may be true that a soft answer turns away wrath (Proverbs 15:1), and there may be times when we need to turn the other cheek (Matthew 5:39). Nevertheless, history teaches us that individually and collectively we must resort to violence in the face of obstinate injustice.

12. **Ukrainian misstep:** When it comes to war, a rule of thumb is not to telegraph your intentions ahead of your actions. Announcing an offensive blitz months before it occurs is not a profile in wisdom. That would be the equivalent of Japan telling the U.S. their intention to attack Pearl Harbor long before the strike. Of course, I understand that the political and military circumstances surrounding the Ukrainian/Russian conflict may have triggered this giveaway strategy. Still . . .

13. **An Oppenheimer reprieve:** People don't realize that when our B-29s fire-bombed the city of Tokyo on the night of 9-10 March 1945, those incendiary bombs killed 100,000 Japanese civilians in a single night. It was one of the most destructive bombing raids in human history. It was at least as destructive as the atomic bomb dropped on Hiroshima

in August of that same year (80,000 civilian casualties with additional radiation deaths). The Tokyo raid also killed more than twice as many civilians than those killed by the A-bomb dropped on Nagasaki. (This E-ism is a repeat from the HISTORY category.)

(Flashback Vol. 1)
The Vietnam War: Between 1965-1974 the estimated combat and civilian fatal casualties totaled 1,353,000 (58,200 were Americans). At its inception the U.S. Congress thought it was doing the right thing, and so did most Americans. In retrospect, it appears we were wrong. I am reminded of the wisdom-words attributed to the Buddha: "A foolish person, even when he wants to do good, may instead do something that leads to destruction."

WOMEN AND MEN

Emergence

In the human deck of cards,
where Jacks and queens
and lofty kings
are found in juxtaposition,
I saw you as the queen of hearts,
without the pomp and circumstance,
awaiting disposition.
But not for me.

I loved you from afar.
Proximity denied.
And yet the pundits say
that the owner of a lonely heart
can still find respite from afar.
But not for me.

*(The remainder of this poem is found
in the "Additional Poems" chapter.)*

1. **Mothers**: Aside from our spectacular universe, a mother's heart is persuasive evidence of God's existence.

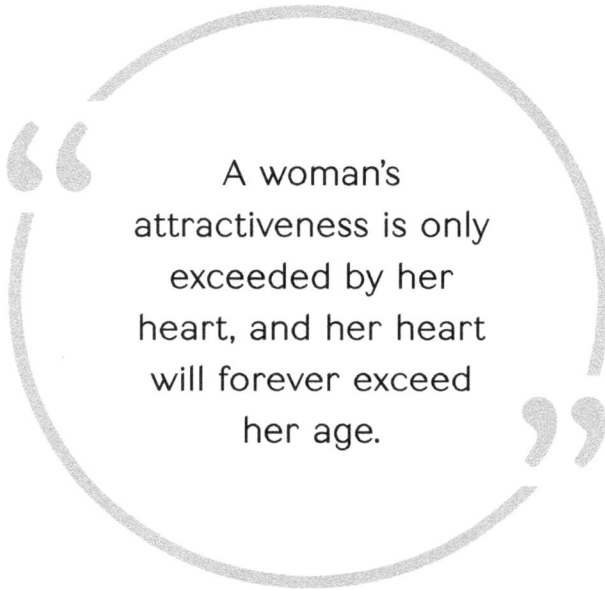

> " A woman's attractiveness is only exceeded by her heart, and her heart will forever exceed her age. "

2. The Declaration of Independence (DI) highlights the following rights and ideals: *We hold these truths to be self-evident, that all men are created equal, that they are endowed by their Creator with certain unalienable Rights, that among these are Life, Liberty and the pursuit of Happiness.* Unfortunately, and I can't prove it, but given the sexist climate of 1776, I hardly think that men thought all of those DI aspirations applied to women— certainly not in terms of "created equal." The turbulent journey for women's rights, including suffrage, lends credence to my skepticism. Sadly, the fight for evenly balanced worth between the sexes remains unfinished. However, I am hopeful

that women will eventually take their rightful place in the pantheon of equality.

3. A woman's attractiveness is only exceeded by her heart, and her heart will forever exceed her age.

4. Most women know what most men are thinking, but men don't know that. But if women really knew what men were thinking, men would know that. Think about it

> " Sadly, the fight for evenly balanced worth between the sexes remains unfinished. However, I am hopeful that women will eventually take their rightful place in the pantheon of equality. "

5. **The manly man:** Bravely facing the unknown is the antithesis of fear that immobilizes. I think that's what President Roosevelt meant when he said those immortal words after Japan's attack on Pearl Harbor: "We have nothing to fear but fear itself." However, sometimes facing the unknown is what gets us killed. That's one of the reasons we fear the unknown.

Although we can accept the nuance of Roosevelt's comment in its given context, the idea that we have nothing to fear but fear itself is a bit misleading. Fear can be an advantageous adrenalin shot, and a defense mechanism against a clear and present danger. Accordingly, macho men need not be ashamed to be afraid.

(Flashback Vol. 1)

I am a man who will be 83 [86] this year. Aside from dying, I've always wondered when the physical urge to be with a woman would end. I'll let you know.

YOUNG FOLKS

Misadventure

When he was young,
he went to sea
to see what he could see.
he heard the captain yell to him,
"Climb up the mast to see."

He took the cue
and climbed the mast,
a bird's-eye view to see.
He did it with agility,
and most excitedly.

A thunderous day
the ship would sway.
So to and fro,
if you must know
he felt the ocean spray.

Atop the mast he saw it all.
he heard the thunder sound.
And before he knew what happened,
He fell overboard and drowned.

1. During an energetic conversation, when someone misses your point, you are likely to say, "You don't understand." That is close to an insult, and it makes the individual defensive. It's better to say, "I haven't made myself clear." That places the onus back on oneself and neutralizes any negative feelings that might arise otherwise.

2. It's excusable to be young without wisdom, but it's inexcusable to be old without it. Hence the proverbial saying, "There's no fool like an old fool."

3. Would you like to grow up to be a mule? Anyone who says education isn't important . . . well, I won't say it. Anyway here's an old song from 1944 that's worth a listen. It's not classical music and it isn't rock and roll, but Bing Crosby has a message for the ages. Shazam! *(Search for "Swinging on a Star" on YouTube with lyrics.)*

4. Take as many steps as you need while on the road to success, as long as no one is being trodden underfoot.

5. Imagine whatever you want to imagine while riding the carousel of imagination. However, if in real life you are able to grasp the brass ring of your imagination, it will not likely be as you imagined.

6. Some elderly people spend more time living in the past than they do in the present. Some young people spend more time living in the future than they do in the present. The former is ok, but the latter is not.

> "
>
> It's excusable to be young without wisdom, but it's inexcusable to be old without it.
>
> "

7. Some people don't realize that one of our most popular proverbs—"One man's meat is another man's poison"—is not applicable to vegetarians. Vegetarians require a slightly modified motto. How about: "One man's vegetable is another man's poison"? Now there's a proverb that even youngsters can understand.

8. When we're young we are very naïve. That's a good thing . . . naïveté is what leads to happy days. If ignorance is bliss, then naïveté must be a close cousin.

9. People seldom realize how precious their youth is until they get long in the tooth.

(Flashback Vol. 1)

For the young: (1) Keep your eyes open and your ears listening for the galloping horse of history; those thundering hoofs seldom come along—sometimes never. But if that thoroughbred comes your way, don't hesitate to hop on; once it's gone, it's gone for good. (2) Latch on to opportunity when it is offered; make your own when it's not. (3) Lead with your brain, consult with your heart, and don't ignore your gut feelings. (4) Never yield when you know you're right, unless it's for the greater good.

SELECTED "ONE-LINERS"
FROM VOLUME I
(A synopsis for your convenience)

The quality of life is predicated on the decisions made prior to the crisis.

Only after we are educated do we come to realize how ignorant we still are.

Explaining the findings of biblical criticism to my college students is like trying to dismantle a spider's web without breaking it.

Right or wrong, whatever one believes can appear to be logically supported.

A collegiate New Testament course is like a hammer: It can build a house or tear one down; it should do both.

Atheism and religious fundamentalism are opposite sides of the same coin, both proffer certitude about the unknowable.

The meaning of life has no meaning unless we become meaningful to others.

Undisciplined minds that cannot differentiate between truth and falsehood are the wrecking balls of a democratic society.

We all have a strong inclination to believe something is true because the people that surround us believe it to be so.

Most people will think inside of the box; a few people can think outside of the box; hardly anyone can think outside of the warehouse.

Beware of beliefs served up on the plate of tribal agreement.

Acts of kindness generated by how one feels is a natural inclination; acts of kindness generated in the absence of feeling is the most telling sign of one's true character.

Blind faith is the Pied Piper that has led believers of every stripe into the bowels of Hell and has fostered doctrinal absurdities that no one in their right mind should accept.

Atheism slams and locks the door to the house of supernatural possibility; agnosticism leaves you a key.

Self-love is the prerequisite for altruism; it is impossible to love others if you cannot love yourself (not to be confused with narcissism).

To treat *all* sentient life forms with kindness—whenever possible—will eventually lead one to experience life at the deepest level of sensitivity.

Yesterday's miracle is owned by the science of today—today's miracle will be owned by the science of tomorrow.

I see spiders as a necessary ecological blessing, but then again, I'm not smaller than they are.

The more you have going for you when death approaches, the less likely you'll feel like going.

Everyone is wrong when it comes to religious belief, or lack thereof; I just hope I'm wrong in the right direction.

A person incapable of expressing kindness should not be considered undeserving of kindness.

Perhaps evolution is the hand of God writing in slow motion.

Most people will march to the beat of a conventional drum; very few will march to the beat of a different drum; fewer yet will become drummers.

If someone plays the God-card as a reason to circumvent the obvious, disengage.

To honor and respect all life forms within the animal kingdom reflects an intuitive grasp of this enigma we call life.

Hopefully, education leads one to a better quality of ignorance.

Adulterous lovers at play in a torrid romance are shipmates on a pleasure cruise, unknowingly speeding toward an island called "Snafu."

The difference between information, misinformation, and disinformation is lost on the masses and, therefore, can lead to a misguided electorate.

Anarchy is the end result of a society lacking civility and manifesting a disregard for the rule of law.

The alignment of one's persona with one's true self is a life-long battle not usually won.

If humanity is the final blueprint of God's highest creation, then "He" needs to go back to the drawing board.

Faith without doubt is shortsighted; doubt without faith is unsighted.

You may argue the point, but you'll never make your point arguing.

The art of teaching young people is meeting them where you find them and by allowing the learning experience to be a two-way street.

If you think that my thinking is sometimes flawed, you'd be right. But if you think yours isn't, you'd be wrong.

The beauty of nurturing a friendship is that the fallout is reciprocal.

Taking things for granted reflects a major absence of both hindsight and foresight.

To be uncaring is a serious form of poverty. To be unkind is a much more severe deficiency.

Everyday miracles don't happen; every day is the miracle!

"You cannot reason but from what you *know,*" and that's why the reasoning of most people is unreasonable.

For the elderly: It would be foolish not to number your days when you know your days are numbered. Get it done!

Temptation should be avoided but yield to it whenever possible.

I can't quite see the Grim Reaper yet, but I can hear his footsteps fast approaching.

One man's woman is another man's desire.

Reality is oblivious to what you opine, and what you opine changes it not.

When we deal with our personal indiscretions, our most perfected remedy resides in the act of self-forgiveness, expertly applied through the refined art of rationalization.

As we seniors approach the abyss, let's hope it's a launching pad, not a crash-and-burn site.

The hardest thing I ever tried to do is to get through life without hurting anyone. I didn't make it.

Earth's ecosystem has yet to decide whether the human animal is a wonder or a blunder.

I prefer to be less enthralled in my "reality" than to ride the roller coaster of evangelical thrills, which I now find wanting and, therefore, unsuited to my true self.

Ignorance may be bliss but it's usually amiss; that makes it a short-term gain but a long-term pain.

We have an almost infinite capacity to rethink matters of all sorts, so that they will come out the way we want them to.

Life has been hard on me. I had to learn from other people's mistakes because I never made any of my own.

Religious and political fanatics are the triggering mechanisms for dangerous stupidity.

The same bottle of Gorilla Glue conjoins the atheist and the fundamentalist believer; they are bonded together by the same inflexible certitude that differs in name only.

A question for people of all faiths: Am I helping to slay the dragon of intolerance, or am I perpetuating the dragon of intolerance?

If my logic is based on a false premise, I have become a rabbit scooting down a rabbit hole from which I cannot be rescued.

The phrase, "God's will," is sometimes a necessary and valuable firewall that shields the emotionally wounded from any combustible alternatives.

We should always try to keep looking at the bright side of life, even when the shadows lengthen as we face the setting sun.

History teaches us that you can muscle people into compliance, but you can't muscle them out of defiance.

I no longer believe in God as traditionally framed, but I do believe in the Mystery that can't be framed.

I wish I didn't know so much about so little, and so little about so much.

Religious belief without some doubt is based on the neurotic disposition of self-deception.

The losses of our mothers, fathers, children, sisters, brothers, and all kinds of others, are the gut-wrenching mentors that teach us empathy beyond sympathy.

I'm not afraid of dying; I'm just afraid of not living longer.

Trying to speak rationally to an opinionated person is like trying to sweep the sand off the beach with a toothbrush.

We're all self-centered; it's only a matter of degree that marks the difference between us.

Disregard and brutality against the "lower" animals is the foundational catalyst that spurs man's disregard and brutality against his own kind.

Scientific and religious adjustments are unstoppable because the ever-evolving expansion of knowledge continues to home in on the most convincing explanations of reality.

Higher education is expensive, but ignorance costs more; therefore, education should cost less.

I never learned how not to be stupid when I fell in love.

Getting your share: Don't worry about hypocrisy; there's more than enough to go around.

Being old doesn't mean you are ineffective—it just means you are not as effectual.

The "fountain of youth" is not a pipe dream; it is the mother of modern science, and that mother is in labor even as I speak.

We should not apply the rules of logic, common sense, or scholarly methodology to other religions if we are not willing to apply them to our own.

In some cases, the lack of *opportunity* for a clandestine affair is one of the main factors that separates the so-called virtuous person from the fallen one.

Don't people understand that when they accuse another person of being a "pain in the ass," they are actually calling themselves an ass?

I wonder if there was a compassionate god looking out for the dinosaurs. If so, I hope it's not the same one we have.

Kindness is the sweet elixir of life, both given and received.

"The emperor has no clothes": Power unveils, and absolute power unveils absolutely.

Trying to sidestep bad karma is like trying to walk between raindrops in a thunderstorm without getting wet

Do we gravitate toward like-minded people because we think them to be as rational as ourselves, or are we gravitating toward like-minded people because they are similarly irrational?

A conspiracy theory thrives and derails where ignorance prevails.

Many a spouse has jumped the fence only to discover that the greener grass was Astroturf.

Before the invention of glasses, midlife divorces were minimal.

Hindsight may be 20/20 but foresight is 20/10.

Be kind—everyone you know and everyone you meet is fighting a battle!

Those who think they know, know not; those who know they know not, know.

Any society that weakens its moral and judicial sentiment will unleash the unbridled hedonistic wants of the powerful few at the expense of the many.

There seems to be a direct correlation between the number of years one has lived and the number of pills one has to take.

If someone believes that they possess the one true religion, they have probably never studied cultural anthropology.

Religious presumption, dogmatism, and the lack of historical knowledge are the obstinate bedfellows of a distorted worldview.

The put-down of science is a long-established pastime for many; it is the celebration of ignorance.

The failure to forgive is a squandered opportunity for momentous self-improvement.

St. Peter, while standing guard at the Pearly Gates, yells out to Lazarus as he approaches: "What! You again?"

History confirms that religions of every stripe can make some people remarkably better, yet others remarkably worse.

Don't let your intellectualism trick you into dismissing supernatural possibility.

Educational glasses do not always bring reality into perfect focus, but they do sharpen it somewhat.

I wasn't born with a silver spoon in my mouth, but there was a spoon.

There's nothing wrong with someone moving the goal posts; the only thing that really matters is the direction in which they move them.

Sadly, many earthlings do not have three numerical digits in their IQ.

Religious and political extremes are, in part, the outcomes of an uneducated society.

Making the wrong choice can be painful; sometimes, making the right choice can be more so.

Members of any society that do not engage the body politic are certain to put themselves at the mercy of those who do.

Wouldn't it be great if I were half as wonderful as others think I am?

Humans may be at the top of the pecking order, but they are also at the top of the mayhem order—a strange side effect of higher intelligence.

Betrayal is like a stealth bomber; you never see it coming.

Cosmic arrogance: Just because we're a grain of sand on the beach doesn't mean we *are* the beach.

As the aging process catches up with us, I take some comfort in knowing that once our usefulness melts away, dying is a contribution to the greater good.

Any individual who is able to think clearly, sensibly, and logically, will be shunned and deemed irrational by the tribe.

High School days and beyond: Some people begin as butterflies and mutate into caterpillars, while others start out as caterpillars and metamorphose into butterflies.

The one thing I cannot tolerate is intolerance!

Voice your intent but promise not, for tomorrow is not promised.

Sometimes social media platforms provide followers with a speedway to an off-ramp that takes them directly to the cross streets of Misinformation and Disinformation.

We've all been fooled at times, often by ourselves.

The problem with common sense is that it's not so common

They say that a high IQ is like underwear—it's not really something you should show off.

I suspect that the prevailing concept of the Devil is actually a nonexistent scapegoat for humanity's dark side.

The mark of a great sitcom is when you no longer hear the laugh track.

Some people are like chameleons—they are wishy-washy individuals who are forever changing color, contingent on circumstance.

The only problem I think I have is thinking I don't have one.

It is strange how religion can screw some people up, and others for the lack of it.

Why is it that my elderly body is so obviously out of sync with my adolescent body, while my elderly mind is so much in tune with my adolescent mind?

In my opinion, an individual who has a photographic memory with an average IQ is sadder than a Greek tragedy.

We are always young enough to make mistakes because we never get too old not to make them.

I find it interesting to feel bad about a past experience, yet feel grateful that it happened.

Necessity may be the mother of invention, but disaster is the mother of mobilization.

Social justice without religion is fine; religion without social justice is not.

Don't try to make every day count. It is a fool's errand and it will wear you out.

Reasoning only within the confines of one's tribal knowledge is usually a one-way ticket to a half-truth (or worse).

Circa 2016-2025: Is it my imagination, or have McCarthyism zombies been resurrected and released into the American bloodstream?

There's nothing more wasteful than time being wasted.

Am I tired of being someone I am, that others think I'm not, or am I tired of being someone I'm not, that others think I am?

There's no vaccine that cures conspiracy gullibility.

The problem with open-minded people is that they have close-minded beliefs (that would be most of us).

SELECTED "ONE-LINERS" FROM VOLUME II
(A synopsis for your convenience)

If we fully understood the *improbability* of our present life, we would be more likely to entertain the *possibility* of an afterlife.

Don't get lost in religiosity; get lost in humanitarianism. The gods will love you for it.

We serve ourselves best when we serve others first.

Will there ever come a time when the term "humankind" will refer primarily to disposition rather than category?

Empathy: If you cannot fill your eyes with tears, you cannot see clearly.

The primary meaning of life is wrapped around the kindness we show to others, even in the absence of reciprocity.

VOTE! If you choose not to vote, just remember this old Spanish proverb: El que calla concede (he who is silent concedes the point).

Animal rights: In the observation of cruelty, a sensitive person will suffer more injury than one whose nature is not so inclined.

If religion is your strong suit, make sure you concentrate on its prime directives of kindness and justice, as opposed to its less impressive directive of fidelity.

It is better for your character to outweigh your good reputation, rather than vice versa.

For some people, feeling bad is their way of feeling good.

Race and gender: Three kinds of people should be treated equally: my kind, your kind, and their kind.

Those who do not understand the animal side of human nature understand neither animals, humans, nor nature.

It's great to have the eye of the tiger and the heart of a lion. But without a heart of gold, an empty shell remains.

Anyone who says, "No one is above the law," and then turns around and says, "but this is an unusual case,"—as if to invoke an exception—contradicts and weakens American jurisprudence.

The occurrence of one's derogatory comments about another is usually in direct proportion to the nobility of one's character.

The moment in which we live is more highly prized if one recognizes that consistency and stability are short-lived.

It's not hard to see that some animals are more like humans than they are animals, while some humans are more like animals than they are humans.

I had to learn from other people's mistakes because I never made any of my own.

To downplay, disparage, or de-emphasize the good side of human nature is to be skewed in the wrong direction.

Most people don't go to the dark side; it's the dark side that comes to them.

The enigmatic nature of love is that we can be accepted despite our shortcomings, and then be rejected for the same reasons when the pixie dust settles.

There's no better way of starting the day than waking up.

Pick any social issue and you'll see that people are the problem . . . but they're also the solution.

Pseudo-reasoning is a self-serving mechanism that we conveniently employ to justify irrational behavior.

The law sees no difference between a VIP and a less privileged person. Yeah, right!

The flame of fame, whatever the sort, whatever the length of time, is mostly relegated to the dustbin of history by the slow-burning candle of impermanence.

Religious belief or unbelief is not the significant difference between people; it's between those who are kind and those who are not.

Sometimes religious rituals tend to metamorphose into perfunctory repetition.

Family is either an orchard of plenty, or a wasteland of familiarity.

Any person who slavishly follows social media platforms is usually a person who is simultaneously guided and misguided but is unable to tell the difference.

It's usually the attitude one takes in the argument that persuades or dissuades.

Some of our politicians are having trouble rising to the level of mediocrity.

The USA vs. worldly mayhem: We often fail to appreciate the luxury of spending a boring evening at home.

Why is it that empathy, wisdom, and kindness, accelerate as our life force decelerates?

If we fail to redefine the freedom of speech in the digital age, the repercussions will be costly?

One man's religion is another man's falsehood.

All carnivorous beings are serial killers.

We can learn from science that a failed experiment is a form of progress.

Similar to a boat without a rudder, or a submarine without ballast, a life without mythos lacks direction and stability.

It's the social and physical sciences that have forced religions to reframe their beliefs, not vice versa.

Not only is history written by the winners, sometimes it's written by the last one standing.

Birds with clipped wings in small cages are another blatant symbol of a societal blind spot.

2025 politics: It is our responsibility to become a clear and present danger to those who have become a clear and present danger.

Righteous indignation provides the perfect excuse for unrighteous behavior.

Boot Hill: Does anybody know where they buried the cowboys who didn't have boots?

Imagine, if you will, what a wonderful world this would be if everyone thought that everybody's child was *everybody's* child.

Ambition: Whether the outcome be success or failure, don't reach for the big enchilada unless you have the stomach for it.

To say that man is created in the image of God is somewhat akin to saying that a donkey is created in the image of man.

Science derails itself when it becomes dogmatic, and that's especially true of religion.

The road to hell may be paved with good intentions, but the road to heaven is paved with good intentions fulfilled.

The only thing more irritating than the mind of a knownothing person is the mind of a know-it-all person.

Like a buoyant cork placed at the depths of the sunless ocean floor, there is nothing that can stop the truth from rising toward the light of day.

Sometimes elderly people looking back on their glory days can see that the glory in those days was specific to their outlook, and of little significance to others.

History is awash with freethinkers that are buried and forgotten in the Avant-garde cemetery.

Stay in your own league—it's hard to hit a homerun in someone else's ballpark.

Those who are unlovable are still loveworthy. And those who can love the unlovable are the most loveworthy.

The fog of war cannot rival the fog of social media!

There are times when our moral compass should be ignored if, in fact, the moral code undermines the ultimate good.

Friendship is the oasis that is found in the desert of loneliness.

Sometimes people will say they're killing time, but it's time that's killing them.

Tribalistic xenophobia and corporate greed may not be the root of all evil, but they certainly are some of the frontrunners.

Science is the mother of designed miracles.

For most people, beliefs are determined by the time capsule in which they are born, along with the herd mentality of their peers.

The needs of the self outweigh the needs of the many, at least in one's own mind.

The dominance of partisan passion over common sense leads to damnable behavior, be it political or religious.

Most people never escape from the internment camp of cultural indoctrination.

It's best not to live at the top of your voice, or at the bottom of your morality.

We are made safe in the public arena by the rule of law and social mores, but we are never safe from another person's thoughts.

My greatness is surpassed only by my humility.

Killing any sentient life form unnecessarily, and with impunity, is the *normalization of cruelty* and, therefore, unrecognized as such.

As I continue to age, it's getting harder to know if I'm still live ammo, or a spent bullet.

Growing up: We were stretched or stunted by the people who surrounded us.

It is better to be perplexed by the uncertainties of open-mindedness than to remain unchallenged by the certainties of close-mindedness.

Every creature that dies by our hand unnecessarily, is an affront to Providence.

I really don't like the idea of old age; there's not much future in it.

The *common man* is never so monstrous as when he is granted permission to be inhuman by a higher authority.

Cause and effect: The will of God is often confused with man's lack of knowledge, coincidence, or the randomness of nature.

The best way to curtail war and mass immigration on planet Earth is through the globalization of prosperity.

Be kind and feel good . . . be kinder and feel better.

Coming and going: No ticket into this life gives you a free ride, and the price of admission varies considerably . . . as it does with the exit portal.

A play on words: Has a man called Nicolas lost more money than a man who is penniless?

Is there a significant difference between a sell-by date and an expiration date? . . . there is if you're old.

Life is a bodily journey between two unknowables.

Tenderhearted tears are the unmasking of the soul; they are the crystal pearls from those who care.

2024: Some people can't see the forest for the trees; some people can't see the trees for the forest; some politicians can't see either.

I am open to religious insights from various traditions, but I am not open to claims of religious supremacy.

Reality is my favorite playground, but not always my favorite comfort zone.

You'll never be alone, no matter how old you get; there'll always be someone around to pick your pocket.

We don't like to admit it, but sometimes getting even is the only path to one's peace of mind.

The easiest thing one does in life is to acquire a bad habit.

Aside from our spectacular universe, a mother's heart is persuasive evidence of God's existence.

Going to a political rally is a bit like going to the movies. To enjoy the event, you must be willing to suspend reality.

Music, laughter, chocolate and friendship are the shock absorbers of life.

It's very taxing to drive down memory lane if you've had a lot of accidents along the way.

The road to heaven is paved with acts of kindness, not belief.

The cataracts of social conditioning and ignorance are excised by education. To what degree depends on the education.

Civil discourse within the body politic has given way to rigor mortis.

The world would be a much better place if people could see it from my perspective, and even more so if I could see it from theirs.

2025: Criminal behavior, criminal law, nationalism, ageism, racism, misogyny, religion, and political partisanship have conflated into a heretofore unimagined national nightmare.

Why conspiracies thrive: A logical argument based on a faulty premise will be just as convincing as one based on a viable one.

Religions don't own the concepts of love and forgiveness, but they far and away lead the pack.

Here are the four words you never hear between Republicans and Democrats when it comes to politics: "You may be right."

Just because you're not educated doesn't mean you're not wise; just because you're educated doesn't mean you are.

I'm wondering if desert *nomads* ever get angry.

In the era of social media, the freedom of speech is more commonly antithetical to the freedom of truth.

Many Americans are less educated than I am, and that worries me. I wonder if I worry those who are more educated than I am.

A woman's attractiveness is only exceeded by her heart, and her heart will forever exceed her age.

2024 Secret Service miscues: Sometimes complacency and carelessness are the byproducts of long-standing tranquility.

One doesn't have to be educated to display common sense; and the fact that one is educated doesn't guarantee that one does.

War: It takes two to tangle, and countless atrocities before it gets untangled.

When tragedy strikes, wisdom and common sense transforms the "why me" bewilderment into a "why not" understanding.

Religion is not the problem . . . religionism is.

For the young: Take as many steps as you need while on the road to success, as long as no one is being trodden underfoot.

To be aware that one is ignorant of one's ignorance is a self-imposed blessing; it is the beginning of humility, and the mitigation of hubris.

If you consider someone to be wise, consider yourself to be wise. Wisdom can only be discerned by those who have it.

Life's journey: Never-ending successions of losing and winning, suffering and well-being, sadness and joy, are the balancing counterpoints that lead to personal growth, if we so choose.

Higher education that excludes the humanity courses—history, ethics, world religions, philosophy, logic, and so forth—could diminish a student's ability to think logically, write cogently, and ponder broadly.

I recently turned 85. Today I am planting seeds and pulling up weeds; tomorrow I'll be pushing up daisies.

In the long run, ignorance never trumps knowledge, but it takes a hell of a toll, nonetheless.

2025 Confirmation hearings: The Senate is derelict in its duty—regardless of the party in charge—if it only kicks the tires but doesn't check the engine.

History continues to demonstrate that reasoning from a position of ignorance or pride can lead individuals, and even nations, to catastrophic consequences.

The sacred web of life: Those who see the interconnectedness of *all* sentient life forms will see themselves in all beings, and thereby avoid the disregarding of animals as others so readily do. There's never a straight line between moral upbringing and immoral behavior.

When it comes to the question of the cosmos, there can be only two possibilities: Who did it, or what did it?

I never watched *Little House on the Prairie* without a box of Kleenex nearby.

When a con man waves hello or shakes your hand, just remember—there's a middle finger in there somewhere.

Recognizing our own hypocrisy, although quite visible to others, is like trying to spot germs without a microscope.

If you do something wrong and fall into a deep hole, look up to the people who can toss you a rope.

Despite some serious side effects, including a one-way ticket to Palookaville, growing old is a privilege.

Time, curiosity, ingenuity, logic, and the scientific method are the filters that separate truth from falsity, innovation from stagnation.

Birds and butterflies are Mother Nature's materialized rainbows.

A man who is full of himself is truly empty.

Ancient theology is today's mythology—will today's theology be tomorrow's mythology?

The aging process places locks on the doors of opportunity—except for the door with the exit sign.

Maybe someone should take the blindfold off Lady Justice so she can see what she's doing.

America is awash with books that are becoming the symbolic tombstones of America's literary graveyard.

To be untruthful for the sake of another, at the expense of one's own integrity, makes for a difficult decision.

The terms hunting and fishing are euphemisms for killing.

A cliché with supplement: "The tough get going when the going gets tough," but the smart stop going when the going is insurmountable.

The most essential prerequisite for exploring the spiritual realm is the elimination of certitude.

To be disrespected carries a load; to be well-regarded carries a load of its own.

ABOUT THE AUTHOR

Hollywood: During the early 1960s, while pursuing his university and seminary education, Ernie founded a rock group that came to be known as the Rip Chords. They were joined by Columbia producer Terry Melcher (son of Doris Day) and Bruce Johnston (who later joined the Beach Boys when the Rip Chords disbanded). The Rip Chords placed five singles on Billboard's Hot 100 chart, 1963-65 (see: erniebringas.com or Wikipedia article). Their music can be accessed on YouTube, iTunes, Spotify, and other platforms.

Ministry & Music: After graduating from seminary, Ernie was ordained as a minister of the United Methodist Church and worked primarily with high school and college age youths. While working at the church in Cupertino, CA (1969-75), he encountered some young people with exceptional music skills. He harnessed their vocal and songwriting talents and founded a singing group he called Homestead and Wolfe (named after the cross streets of the church he was serving). Eventually he took the group to Hollywood for a recording session at the preeminent Gold Star Studios. Having recorded at Columbia Records with the Rip Chords, he used his friends from the Wrecking Crew (renowned Hollywood studio musicians) to provide the instrumental tracks. The end result was an album titled Our Times (aka The Gold

Star Tapes 1973-75). High praise for this album came from many quarters. It was reissued in 2004 as a CD with six new additional songs. Ernie sang with the group and wrote nearly all of the lyrics. Most of the tunes came from JoAnne Avery Neish and Brian Gundy. (See: homesteadwolfe.com)

HBO Max, FX and STARZ: Fast forward to 2022-23. Two songs from the *Our Times* Homestead and Wolfe album were used on three separate networks. (1) On March 20th, 2022, the song "King of the Mountain" was included in the HBO Max mini-series titled *"Winning Time: The Rise of the Lakers Dynasty."* (2) Another album cut "Do I Love You?" aired on March 24th. It was included in the FX TV series *Atlanta* for episode 302 titled "Sinterklaas Is Coming To Town." (3) On September 6th, 2023, that song also aired on STARZ TV American comedy series *Minx* for episode 206 titled "This Is Our Zig."

Transition: Ernest Bringas, Jr. (aka Ernie Bringas) served the United Methodist Church for almost twenty years before venturing into academia. As an adjunct faculty member, Ernie taught Religious Studies—World Religions; Introduction to the New Testament—at Glendale Community College in Arizona for twenty-one years. Under their auspices, he also taught these courses at ASU (Arizona State University) for a few years.

Rainbow Ridge Books publishes spiritual, metaphysical, and self-help titles, and is distributed by Square One Publishers in Garden City Park, New York.

To contact authors and editors, peruse our titles, and see submission guidelines, please visit our website at www.rainbowridgebooks.com.